Shakespeare's London w[...] some familiar urban pr[...] influx of people from t[...] areas, unemployment, inadequate housing, poverty, lack of medical care, and widespread crime.

The Parish of St. Botolph without Aldgate, a microcosm of London, stood close to the City wall. *Chronicle from Aldgate* is based on a study of the parish's record books— records not previously published. Unlike most parish registers of that time, those kept by the clerks of St. Botolph's are surprisingly detailed. They list the deaths and burial dates of individuals and often their ages, addresses, and occupations, supposed causes of death, and various burial charges. Summaries of coroners' inquests in many cases of violent or accidental death are included, as are notations of banns, christenings, excommunications, alms collected for the poor—even some historical events.

The records permit a unique demographic study of annual christenings and burials; infant and child mortality rates; frequency of fatal accidents, homicides, executions, and suicides; and the death tolls in four epidemics of plague. But *Chronicle from Aldgate* is much more than a statistical record. For example, it elucidates some Elizabethan ideas about disease and its causes, and describes an effective system of public assistance at the parish level. The records offer a unique glimpse into urban life that will be of particular interest to specialists in public health, European history, and medical history.

Mr. Forbes, author of *The Midwife and the Witch,* is professor of anatomy at the School of Medicine, Yale University.

Chronicle from Aldgate

New Haven and London

Yale University Press

1971

Chronicle from Aldgate

LIFE AND DEATH IN

SHAKESPEARE'S LONDON

BY THOMAS ROGERS FORBES

Published with assistance from the foundation
established in memory of Philip Hamilton McMillan
of the Class of 1894, Yale College.
Copyright © 1971 by Yale University.
Library of Congress catalog card number: 75–140528
International standard book number: 0–300–01386–8

Designed by Sally Sullivan
and set in Linotype Garamond type.
Printed in the United States of America by
The Carl Purington Rollins Printing-Office
of the Yale University Press.

Distributed in Great Britain, Europe, and Africa by
Yale University Press, Ltd., London; in Canada by
McGill-Queen's University Press, Montreal; in Mexico
by Centro Interamericano de Libros Académicos,
Mexico City; in Central and South America by
Kaiman & Polon, Inc., New York City; in Australasia
by Australia and New Zealand Book Co., Pty., Ltd.,
Artarmon, New South Wales; in India by UBS Publishers'
Distributors Pvt., Ltd., Delhi; in Japan by
John Weatherhill, Inc., Tokyo.

For my parents

Contents

Illustrations

Tables

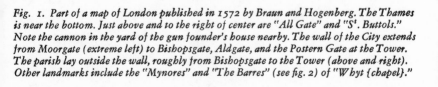

Fig. 1. Part of a map of London published in 1572 by Braun and Hogenberg. The Thames is near the bottom. Just above and to the right of center are "All Gate" and "S^t. Buttols." Note the cannon in the yard of the gun founder's house nearby. The wall of the City extends from Moorgate (extreme left) to Bishopsgate, Aldgate, and the Postern Gate at the Tower. The parish lay outside the wall, roughly from Bishopsgate to the Tower (above and right). Other landmarks include the "Mynores" and "The Barres" (see fig. 2) of "Whyt {chapel}."

y͂ Goouuefowuders h͠

St brutols

The Barres   Whrt

Mₜₜₜₜₜ
rcs.

Postern Gate

THE   TOWRE   Beere howse

attle bvalac   Beere howse

Preface

Among the many treasures of the Guildhall Library in London is a series of record books maintained by the clerks of the Parish of St. Botolph without Aldgate from 1558 until 1625 and beyond. The records are of great interest because, unlike the usual parish registers with their simple lists of births, banns, marriages, and burials, the volumes kept by Thomas Harrydance and his colleagues are a kind of daybook for the parish. The volumes list, for example, not only the name of someone who died in the parish and the date of his burial but usually also his age, address, and occupation, the supposed cause of death, and the various burial charges. If the death were due to violence or accident, a "crowners quest," or coroner's inquest, was held in the church; the findings are summarized in the record. Also carefully set down are notations of alms collected for the poor of the parish and for needy strangers with "licenses," or letters of authorization, notations of banns and churchings, of sermons preached, of visitations by the bishop or his representative (with itemized lists of the costs of the elaborate banquets served afterward), and of the annual perambulations of the parish. Here one can read the notes on penances performed and on a long lawsuit between the parish and a property owner, and here are the records of the dreadful epidemics of plague that smote the parish as they did the rest of the City and the land. The clerks were remarkably well informed about the doings and misdeeds of the congregation. Clerical indignation sometimes thrust aside discretion to castigate unwed parents or lazy rogues in scorching marginal notes.

These were the days of Elizabeth I and James I. St. Botolph's was part of the London of Will Shakespeare. It lay close to the City wall, the Tower, and the mighty Thames. Sailors from the ships trod the parish streets, brawled in its taverns, and sometimes died and were buried in its graveyard, along with artisans and merchants, husbands and wives, infants and centenarians, and pirates hanged at nearby Wapping Dock. It was a poor but lively community, crowded with skilled and unskilled workmen and their families. As one reads the strange Elizabethan script there emerges from the pages a strong image of the all-knowing, conscientious clerk and the people of the parish and their journeys to the church for christening, marriage, communion, for meetings of the vestry, for collections to aid the needy, and finally for committal to the earth while the knell was tolled. Like most such records, the accounts often omit much wanted information and set down many items of little interest, but from it all one can by careful reading, transcription, tabulation, and comparison derive an outline, or better, of life and death in the parish, of ideas of disease, of the incidence of stillbirth and various kinds of accidents, of the parish's obligation and methods to care for the indigent sick, and of many other matters.

Our concern will be chiefly with aspects of birth, sickness and its problems, and death and its causes—all against the background of the parish. By modern demographic standards the information one can extract from the ancient volumes is woefully incomplete. However, as we shall see, in the time of Elizabeth detailed city parish records like those of St. Botolph's were almost nonexistent. The weekly bills of mortality for the City of London, with a few exceptions, have not survived from earlier than 1603. The first census was taken in England only in 1801. Thus any firsthand, regularly collected data on christenings, burials, age at death, and so on beginning in 1558 and continuing through the first quarter of the seventeenth century should be of considerable importance. The St. Botolph records regularly report the "cause" of death for the years 1583 through 1599. This was not done elsewhere until about 1607 and then only briefly, the practice not being resumed until 1624. Some areas of our picture are blurred and others are blank, but much of it is reasonably clear nonetheless. This appears to be the first such study of St. Botolph's and probably of any other London parish in the days of Elizabeth and James.

My debt is very great to Godfrey W. Thompson, F.L.A., Librarian, City of London Libraries, Guildhall Library; to his able and always obliging staff; and particularly to Albert E. J. Hollaender, F.S.A., F.R.Hist.S., Keeper of Manuscripts, Guildhall Library. It was he who told me of the records kept by the parish clerks of St. Botolph without Aldgate and who pointed out the unique features of these volumes. He helped me learn to read Elizabethan handwriting, explained many technicalities, and gave cheerfully and without stint of his time and his scholarship. It is a pleasure also to acknowledge my debt to Professors George Rosen and Colin White of the Yale University School of Medicine who encouraged me, generously read the manuscript, and shared freely their knowledge and skill. I am grateful to the Guildhall Library and the Yale University Map Collection for permitting and assisting in the reproduction of pages from the records, bills of mortality, and maps.

My research in London and New Haven was supported by Grants 1 RO1 LM 00019 and 5 RO1 LM 00570 from the National Library of Medicine, Public Health Service, Department of Health, Education, and Welfare.

New Haven, Connecticut　　　　　　　　　　　　　　　T.R.F.
January 1970

I: The Parish and the People

When Elizabeth I came to her throne in 1558 the ancient City of London was still surrounded on three sides by a wall; the Thames flowed by on the south or fourth side. The City was crowded, and houses were spreading into the open country outside, particularly to the north and west. The settled areas just beyond the wall were known as liberties, their outer limits being marked by bars of iron set into the streets (Harben 1918). So we read, for example, of Whitechapel Bars, and these structures are shown in the delightful semipictorial maps of about 1570 and later (Agas 1905; Braun and Hogenberg 1572). Daniel Defoe in his fictional *Journal of the Plague Year* (1920), written in 1722, remarks, "I lived without Aldgate, about midway between Aldgate Church and Whitechapel

Bars." Beyond the liberties lay open spaces—Moorfields, Spitalfields, East Smithfield. (See figs. 1 and 2.)

The City had, and has, an area of just over a square mile. Its wall was pierced by gates—Ludgate, Newgate, Aldersgate, Cripplegate, Moorgate, Bishopsgate, Aldgate, and, where the wall ended at the Tower, the Postern Gate. Just outside the eastern portion of the wall the long but narrow Ward of Portsoken extended for half a mile northwest and southeast, down toward Tower Hill (Strype 1754; Thornton et al. 1793). At the center of the Ward the Parish Church of St. Botolph without (i.e., outside) Aldgate stood close to the gate of that name. The church was so called to distinguish it from others in the City also dedicated to the saint (Harben 1918; Williams 1960).

The Parish of St. Botolph without Aldgate in 1603 occupied only 45 acres (Angus 1854), or about $\frac{1}{14}$ of a square mile. Its boundaries shifted in later centuries, probably in part as the parish grew. It consisted in Elizabethan days of an "Upper End," north of the church, and a "Lower End" pushing down toward the Tower. It appears that the Upper End coincided roughly with the Ward of Portsoken (12 August 1597),[1] while the Lower End included the Liberty of Eastsmithfield (26 April 1622; Williams 1960). The parish was also divided into four precincts, Houndsditch Precinct, the Precinct next Aldgate, the Pre-

1. References consisting only of a day, month, and year are to entries in one of the parish record books.

cinct next to the Bars, and the Precinct next to Tower Hill (25 April 1617).

The parishes of England, ecclesiastical units in the Middle Ages, came in the sixteenth century also to play a role in the operations of government. The shift followed the uprooting, after the Act of Supremacy in 1534, of the monasteries that had once provided some, though far from adequate, food and shelter for the hungry and homeless. Poverty was massive and appalling in the land, and the state was obliged to take action. Parliament presented the problem to the parishes, thus involving them in civil affairs (Lunt 1957; Trotter 1919). How the parishes responded will be outlined in a later chapter.

A recent study of the status in 1695 of parishes within the City has confirmed that the Parish of St. Botolph without Aldgate was very poor (Glass 1966). In the sixteenth century it was no less impoverished. The parish was crowded as well, even though open fields lay nearby. Poor people could not afford to build houses and were obliged to crowd into available tenements and other inexpensive dwellings. Dirt and disease were commonplace (Wilson 1927). The population was mostly native, although there is occasional mention in the record books of French and Dutch immigrants. The burials of several Negroes are reported.

Christopher Capperbert a blackemoore. [25 October 1586][2]

2. Original spellings and punctuation, often erratic, are usually retained in direct quotations. In a few cases they have been silently modernized to make meanings clear.

Suzanna Pearis a blackamoore tenant to John Despinois. [20 August 1593]

Symon Valencia a Blackamoore. [20 August 1593[3]]

Cassangoe A blacke A moore tenant to Mrs Barbor. [8 October 1593][4]

Easfanyyo a neagar servant to Mr Thomas Barbor a mer-chaunt. [8 October 1593]

A Negar whose name was suposed to be Frauncis. he was servant to Mr Peter Miller a beare brewer dwelling at the signe of the hartes horne in the libertie of Eastsmithfield. [3 March 1596]

Anne bause a Black-more wife to Anthonie bause trom-petter. [10 April 1618]

A Blackamoore woman that died in the street, named Marie. [4 November 1623]

John Come quicke A Blacke-Moore so named, servant to Thomas Love a Captaine. [26 November 1623]

East Indians also lived in the parish: "James (an Indian) servant to Mr James Duppa Beerebrewer" (8 September 1618).

We know the occupation of most of the adults who are mentioned in the record books because this information was regularly included by the clerk as part of his identifica-

3. A plague year.
4. M^r and M^{rs} were abbreviations for Master and Mistress.

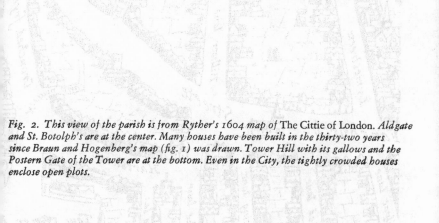

Fig. 2. This view of the parish is from Ryther's 1604 map of The Cittie of London. *Aldgate and St. Botolph's are at the center. Many houses have been built in the thirty-two years since Braun and Hogenberg's map (fig. 1) was drawn. Tower Hill with its gallows and the Postern Gate of the Tower are at the bottom. Even in the City, the tightly crowded houses enclose open plots.*

Peticote Lane

White Cha[pel]

[A]ldgate

Minores

Rosmary la:

East Smith feild

tion of individuals. Other information often recorded was age, the street or lane where the subject lived, and the owner of the house in which the individual dwelt. As a sample from the parish there follows a partial list of the occupations or, alternatively, of the status (i.e., "Gentleman") of fathers whose children were christened during the twelve months from 2 January 1599 to 31 December 1600.[5] The number of men listed for each occupation is also indicated. The spelling, but not the name, of the trade has been modernized.

There were 242 christenings in 1600. The list below ac-

Sailor	17	Blacksmith	4	Painter	3
Cooper	12	Bricklayer	4	Pewterer	3
Tailor	10	Chandler	4	Saddler	3
Silk weaver	9	Shoemaker	4	Tallow chandler	3
Butcher	8	Cordwainer[7]	3	Tipler	3
Drayman	8	Currier[8]	3	Brewer	2
Not stated	8	Felt maker	3	Card maker	2
Carman[6]	7	Girdler	3	Chapman	2
Carpenter	5	Gunmaker	3	Clothworker	2
Gunsmith	5	Haberdasher	3	Cloth maker	2
Porter	5	Joiner	3	Embroiderer	2

5. In Elizabethan times the first day of the year was not 1 January but 25 March. Thus, in the above-mentioned sampling period 24 March 1599 was succeeded by 25 March 1600. Unless otherwise specified all dates in this book will be given in their original form.

6. A cart driver.

7. A worker in cordovan leather.

8. One who dressed leather.

Gentleman	2	Lawyer	2	Schoolmaster	2
Glover	2	Merchant	2	Smith	2
Goldsmith	2	Minstrel	2	White baker[10]	2
Horn breaker[9]	2	Sawyer	2		

counts for 180 of the fathers and suggests the commonest trades. The male parents of the remaining children had other trades, no two of them identical. These and many additional occupations appearing elsewhere in the records may now be considered. It is, of course, almost impossible to select categories into which every occupation will fit neatly. Also, because the clerks did not have a standardized list, the designations they used, e.g., *fishmonger* and *fishwife,* sometimes overlap.

First was a group of professions requiring some degree of education—attorney, lawyer, solicitor for law, pettifogger,[11] curate, minister, monk, doctor of divinity, preacher, swaddler,[12] clerk, scrivener,[13] apothecary, physician, doctor, surgeon, barber-surgeon, poet, pursuivant,[14] schoolmaster (also known as an informer), and scholar. Some of these men had assistants, such as lawyers' clerks, beadles, underbeadles, and sextons. At the professional fringe were the barber and midwife, while the so-called doctors of physic and professors of

9. One who broke animal horn so that it could be made into spoons, combs, etc., by a horner.
10. A man who baked with white flour.
11. A petty legal practitioner.
12. Uncertain, perhaps a Methodist preacher.
13. A public writer, notary.
14. A kind of herald.

physic were almost certainly quacks. There were public officials in varying degree—alderman's deputy, officer at the Custom House, writer in the Custom House, sergeant-at-mace,[15] letter post for France, messenger to Her Late Majesty, bailiff, prison keeper, warden at the Tower.

Because St. Botolph's was close to the Thames, it is not surprising that a good many rivermen and seafarers made their homes in the parish. We find mentioned sailors, masters of ships, pilots, ship's gunners, and ship's boys. There were hoy[16] men and wherrymen and watermen. Nautical suppliers included the compass maker, chandler, sailmaker, hemp dresser, and rope maker. Transportation on land of course was also very important, and so there were the hostler, farrier, horsekeeper, and keeper of hackney horses, the coachman, hackneyman, wagon driver, carman, and drayman, the blacksmith, saddler, spurrier, bit maker, harness maker, maker of furniture for cart horses, horse-collar maker, the wheelwright, and the coach maker.

The military was represented by captains, soldiers, yeomen of the guard, and drummers. A man described as a fencer probably made his living by teaching this skill. There were bowyers,[17] bowstring makers, fletchers,[18] and crossbow makers. Gunpowder had come into use, and as a result there was the powder maker, shot maker, gun founder, gunsmith, gun-

15. A minor police official in the City.
16. A small boat.
17. They made bows (for arrows, not ladies).
18. Arrow makers; also, men who feathered arrows.

maker, snaphance[19] maker, and firelock maker. And there
was still employment for armorers.

An entry for 23 September 1622 makes reference to "the
silk mills," but it is not clear whether they were in the Parish
of St. Botolph. Certainly several skills were required just to
produce this fabric—silk winder,[20] twister, thruster, and
weaver. Many other textile workers lived in the parish,
among them weavers, velvet weavers, linen weavers, fustian[21]
weavers, tuftaffeta weavers, felt makers, cloth makers, pack-
thread makers, thread winders and twisters and dyers, wool
winders, dyers, drawers upon linen cloth, and loom makers.
Textiles and other materials were converted into articles of
clothing by tailors, embroiderers, collar makers, stock makers,
buckle makers, point[22] makers, hot-pressers, glovers, girdlers,
and hosiers. To supply these producers there were button
makers, buttonmold makers, shear makers, pinmakers,
needle makers, horn breakers and horners, starch makers and
soapmakers. For the final touch there were perfumers and
looking-glass makers. Hat makers, hat trimmers, and hatband
makers played their roles, as did shoemakers, cobblers, and
blacking[23] men and their suppliers—the tanners, gray taw-
yers,[24] curriers, and cordwainers.

The production and sale of food were important. St.

19. A gun with a spring lock and flint.
20. He unwound the silk from the cocoon.
21. A cotton and linen cloth.
22. A tie or string to join various garments.
23. For boots and shoes.
24. A kind of tanner.

Botolph's was an urban community, so few agricultural workers lived there, although mention is made of shepherds, hogmen, fowlers, graziers, countrymen, hackers,[25] husbandmen, and gardeners. Some of their products went to the cheesemonger, the victualler, the butcher and his clerk, the bacon seller, the poulterer, the vinegar maker, the costermonger,[26] and the fruiterer. Then there were the fisherman, the fishmonger, and the fishwife. The meal ground by the oatmeal maker and miller and undermiller, the corn sold by the cornmeter[27] and carried by the corn porter, and the fascinating handiwork of the garbler[28] of spices were used by the cook, the baker, the brown baker, the white baker, the sugar baker,[29] and the cake baker. Lest men grow thirsty there were vast labors by the water-bearer, brewer, ale brewer, maltman, underbrewer, beer clerk, vintner, wine porter, distiller of waters, aqua vitae distiller, and aqua vitae seller, aided by the can maker, tankard maker, firkin[30] man, tun[31] man, cooper, tipler,[32] and tapster. Inns, as distinguished from taverns, were operated by innkeepers, while homes were owned by householders and were sometimes supervised by male housekeepers.

25. Various meanings, perhaps men who hacked or hoed the ground.
26. A seller of fruit and vegetables from a street stand or barrow.
27. He measured corn.
28. Mixer.
29. A confectioner.
30. A small wooden cask.
31. A large wooden cask.
32. Tavern keeper.

London was growing steadily. The construction, maintenance, and equipment of buildings called for the skills of the
carpenter, bricklayer, freemason,[33] plasterer, paver, glazier,
locksmith, graver in marble, sergeant[34] painter, the sawyer,
pitman,[35] deal-board seller, millwright, joiner, turner, and
carver and inlayer, the bell founder, mat maker, nail maker,
clock smith, tapestry maker, upholsterer, ladder maker, chim-
ney sweep, and mender of old chairs. There were other men
skilled in the manufacture of useful objects—edge-tool
makers, file cutters, makers of instruments, pump makers,
wiredrawers, sieve makers, basket weavers, inkhorn makers,
tinkers, pot makers, potters, brush makers, paper makers,
founders, braziers,[36] and cutters. There was a scattering
of merchants and tradesmen, factors and brokers,[37] col-
liers and coalmeters,[38] mercers,[39] merchant tailors, haber-
dashers, linen-drapers, ironmongers, woodmongers, fellmon-
gers,[40] stationers, wax-chandlers and tallow chandlers, sellers
of meal, sellers of earthen vessels, sellers of old wooden stuff,
chapmen,[41] and peddlers.

Tobacco and tobacco pipes are not mentioned until about

33. A skilled itinerant mason.
34. Chief.
35. He worked in a sawpit.
36. Brass workers.
37. Dealers and middlemen. Brokers specialized in secondhand
goods.
38. Coal dealers.
39. Dealers in fabrics.
40. Dealers in skins, especially sheepskins.
41. Hawkers.

1612, although they probably were first brought to England in 1565. Pipe smoking became rather popular, necessitating the new skills of tobacco dresser, tobacco seller, and pipe maker. Goldsmiths, gold-wire drawers, and diamond cutters helped to produce jewelry, picture makers practiced their art, musicians, minstrels and players entertained, and card makers and dice makers provided still other means of distraction. Such amenities were usually beyond the purses of the numerous unskilled inhabitants of St. Botolph's Parish. They were the laborers, loaders, and porters, the maidservants and servingmen, and the night man.[42]

Some individuals were identified by status rather than occupation, presumably because they were not employed. Thus we read of knights, esquires, and gentlemen, of single men, bachelors, and strangers, of innocents,[43] of gentlewomen, wives, widows, maidens, old maids, and singlewomen.[44] There were poor men, pensioners, and almsmen,[45] nurse children,[46] common drunkards and roisterers, and, at the very edge of the law or beyond, beggars, masterless men, rogues, and vagrants.

Occasional parishioners must have worked in other parts of London, like the yeoman of the guard, whose duties un-

42. He removed night soil.
43. Mentally retarded individuals.
44. Prostitutes. Respectable unmarried women were *old maids*. The former seem to have been more numerous.
45. Those who received alms.
46. Foster children.

doubtedly took him to Westminster. Some served far away—
in the army, on merchantmen, on the Queen's ships. Some
never came home, but others returned, like "John Shipprey a
poore fellow, that was prest [taken by a press gang] for a
Souldier & Died in Artillerie lane" (1 January 1624), or
David Stephens, cooper, "newlye come home from the East
India" (25 June 1614).[47] Presumably some persons who
worked in the parish made their homes elsewhere.

James Tunstall seems to have had an avocation; he was
described as "citt[izen] & saddler of London & a player" (10
December 1599). Other men enjoyed some prominence as
performers. William Pavy was a player in the Prince's company (8 September 1608). Lodovic Bassano was "one of the
Queens ma^ties [Majesty's] musitions" (18 July 1593). Perhaps Bassano knew Roger Rafton, "a Mad-brayn'de fellow of
Hounsditch, free [member of the Guild] of Musitions" (29
June 1618), or Robert Wroth or Robert Benton, both of
them King's trumpeters (12 August, 20 November 1619).

Walter Anthony Duffield, "beerebrewer A householder
[owner] Alwayes godlye bent unto the poore" (23 October
1589), must have been both well-to-do and generous. Noteworthy clerical figures, in addition to several curates, included
"Christianne Hamor dutchman sometymes [once] a Monnke"
(24 January 1599), "Jasper Dias a bishopp of Ebora in
portingall [Evora, Portugal]" (3 August 1589), and "John
Flood Gentelman Doctor of Divinitie" (3 August 1603).

47. The parish clerks did not actually use the ampersand, but
another symbol also meaning *and*.

And of course there were less admirable souls, at least in the clerk's eyes—"Joane Beldam a lewd person" (30 July 1618), "John Bayart a (Runnygate) Carman" and "Thomas Read a Runnygate Taylor" (3 August 1618), "Robert Dabbs a Newgate bird" (22 September 1618), "John Clarke, a Shifting fellow, of Rosemarie Lane" (15 March 1618), "Thomas Smith, a Runnygate fellow who went a way from his wife" (8 July 1622). And some had simply fallen on evil days.

Sir Hastings Stanley Knigt, lodgeing in Rosemary [Lane] in the house of one Willam Lake, Cook in this parish, was Buryed in the North Churchyard the First day of March Anno domini 1610, who in tymes past had bene a valiant knight, and latelye Fallen in great want, by divers and sundry occasions, which most pacientlye he suffred, makeing a Godly departure.

The morality of the parish was a major concern of the curate. The clerk obviously also felt strongly about moral lapses, but most of the actual evidence for them in the parish records is indirect except for a few entries. Perhaps the clerks were reluctant to sully the account with such an item as the following:

Memorandum that Ellen Wryght of this parish of St Buttolphes without aldgate London being of late presented[48] by the churchwardens of the fore said parish before M^r

48. A presentment was a formal complaint to the bishop or his representative during an official visitation to the parish.

Doctor Stanhope for harboring of a single woman in her
howse named Margerie Adames who was there delivered
of a chyld and the chyld by her carried to the Savoy[49] to be
christned, then convayed a way without punishment for
the which she was inioyned to do pennance for the said
fact, by order for the same taken by Mr Doctor Stanhope
Doctor of the civile Lawe at his chamber on Thursday
being the xv^th day of March 1598. Which pennance was
by her performed & done on Sunday the xviij^th day of
March 1598 in the forenoone after the second lesson before the channcell dore, according to the order of an act
for the same wch order was as followeth.

At this point the clerk quotes Dr. Stanhope's order which
begins with the usual ponderous Latin introduction and then
continues in English. It directs that Ellen Wright

shall on Sunday next at Morning prayer com into her parish church of St Bothulphes Allgate with a white wande in
her hand and there in the middest of the whole congregation uppon her knees shall publiqly with an audible voyce
confesse her fault in harboring a single woman in her
howse named Margery who was there delivered of a chyld,
and the chyld carried by her to the Savoye to be christned
and then the woman convayed a way without punishment
and she shall confesse her selfe to be hartily sorrye for her
said offence and desyre god to forgive her and the people
to pray for her protesting that from hence forthe she will

49. A chapel near the Strand, at some distance from St. Botolph's.

never harbor any more harrlotte or otherwyse offend in the lyke matter hereafter. And of the due and pennetent performance of this pennance in manner and forme aforesaid she is to bring certificate under the Minister and Churchwardens hands subscribed to a coppie of this order unto Christe churche uppon the xxth Day of Aprill next.

Will Blakwell

On 9 September 1599 Agnes Payne was excommunicated "for not being examened [not answering a summons to appear for examination] about a single woman that was delivered of chyld in her howse." An earlier entry (19 January 1583) records the "purgation" of three individuals for immorality.

Royal edicts and historical events often touched the lives of the parishioners. Important announcements were read out during church service; a few were recorded by the clerk.

Memerandum that the minister ded give warning unto the parishioners on Sunday being the xvijth day of august anno 1595. That they weare willed by vertue of a warrant or precept from the commissioners for the said purpose that everie howsholder should prepare to have in a redines bowes and arrowes for them selves there servands and children from the age of vij yeares to the age of lx yeares according to the Tennor of an act made by King henrie the eyght.

Regrettably, there is no explanation why Henry's ancient

edict was being enforced. The requirement that seven-year-old children be armed seems a bureaucratic triumph.

Even more curious was an edict from the mayor of the City of London, read out by the minister of St. Botolph's on 1 June 1595.

By the Maior

To the Alderman
of Portsoken

Where her ma.^{ties} most gratious comandement hath bene signefied unto me that her ma^{ties} pleasure is that no blewe starch shalbe used or worne by any of her ma.^{ties} subjects whatsoever These therfore shalbe in her Maties name strayghtly to chardge and comande you that you cause the beadle[50] of youre ward to repayre to the dwelling howse of everie Inhabytant within the same & to give everye of them strayght charge and comandment in her Maties name that from henceforthe none of them upon payne of her Maties Indignation presume to weare in any of there Ruffes or bands any starche called blewe starche And to the end so that her Maties pleasure hearein may be the better knowne you shall cause the parson or minister of everie severall parish within your ward openly to declare the contents heareof upon Sonday next in the tyme of Devyne service, wherof se you fayle not at y^r perill geven at my Mansion house London, xxviijth of May 1595.

Sebright

50. A minor parish officer who carried out orders received from the vestry meeting.

The basis for the royal command is not at all clear. Richard Steele later was to comment in *The Englishman* (Blanchard 1955) that "the renowned Queen *Elizabeth* was a mortal enemy to the Use of blue Starch in making up Linnen," but he did not know why. Since the proclamation specified "any starche called blewe starche," there may have been no objection to white starch. The blue variety was fashionable in the sixteenth century. Another possibility is that the restriction on the use of starch was an antiplague measure. Mullett (1956) says that the appearance of plague at East Greenwich led Sir John Hawkins, renowned sea captain and chief official of the Admiralty, to undertake preventive measures. One of these was that the council of the adjoining town of Deptford was to stop local production of starch because it involved the use of large numbers of hogs. Hogs were regarded as "a noisome kind of cattle" that might attract the plague. Mullett also notes that in 1622 the council of London reissued restrictions on starch production near places where people lived. It seems just possible that Elizabeth's command of 1595 that blue starch not be *worn* was also an effort to restrict starch manufacture with its attendant supposed danger to the public health. There had been a severe epidemic of plague two years earlier.

A new edict from the mayor on blue starch was read in the church about a year later, on 27 June 1596. Elizabeth was very annoyed that her earlier command was being disregarded:

Her Matie being informed and so hath lately signefied unto me by message from her owne accownte that dyvers persons within this cittie not regarding her highnes said comanndement have & do still in most contemptious sorte use blewe starche whereat she is highly offended, and hath comannded that a present reformation be had by all manner of persons whatsoever within this cittie liberties & suburbes.

No inhabitant of the ward should

thence forthe contemptiously presume to use any blewe starche in any of there linnen openly to be worne abowte there bodies upon payne not only of her Maties displeasure but Imprisonment of their bodies during hir highnes pleasure whereof see you fayle not at your perill.

The Protestant parish did not regret the execution of Mary Queen of Scots. On 9 February 1586 there was "Ringinge for Ieoye [joy] that the queene of skotte was beheaded." A few days later, the clerk notes, the funeral of Sir Philip Sidney—courtier, soldier, author, statesman—"was sollemmized in powles [St. Paul's Cathedral] ye 16th daye of febrewarie 1586." Another historical note is a

Memerandum that Doctor Lopus the traytor to god and the Queenes Matie was Arayned of most high treason at the guild hall the xxviij^th Day of Februarie Ano 1593 being on a thursday.

The reference is to an unfortunate Portuguese, Dr. Rode-rigo Lopez, a prominent London doctor who had become chief physician to the Queen in 1586. He had come to England in 1559 and within ten years had been made a member of the Royal College of Physicians. Although of Jewish birth, he was a Christian. He became involved with prominent members of Elizabeth's court, and in 1593 was accused of being party to a plot to poison her. Charged with treason, Lopez was taken to the Tower in January 1594. A month later he was tried, found guilty, and sentenced to death. It is thought that the Queen doubted his guilt, for she refused for many weeks to sign his death warrant. In the end she did so, swayed perhaps by the anti-Semitism of the populace, and on 7 June Lopez went to the scaffold at Tyburn, protesting his innocence to the end (Lee 1909; Zeman 1965). The whole grim affair may have helped to inspire Shakespeare's *Merchant of Venice* (Craig 1932).

A month after Lopez's arraignment there was a Royal Progress down the Thames.

Memorandum that the Queenes ma^tie ded go to greene-witche from hampton court the xxvj^th Day of Marche ano 1594 by water at wch tyme I spent upon the Ringers iiij^d.

That is, the clerk paid the bell ringers of St. Botolph to make a joyful noise as the Queen's barge slid downstream not far from the church.

There are entries in several years to mark the annual celebration of King James's escape from the Gunpowder Plot; for example,

> on the Fift of November at Night, There was a Sermon in our church, & Thanksgiving for the Kings Maiesties deliverance, and States of yᵉ land, from the Gunpowder Treason.

The death of James and accession of Charles I on 27 March 1625 are respectfully recorded.

> On Sunday the 27 day of this Moneth, our late soveraigne Lord King James departed this mortall life, at his Manour house of Theobaudes in Hartford-shire and on the same day, The Illustrious Prince Charles his Sonne, was proclaymed King of this Kingdome, whom Almightie God long preserve, amongst us, to the Glories of his holie name, and the ioy and comfort of all his subiectes.

This, then, was the Parish of St. Botolph without Aldgate, and these were its inhabitants. It was a poor, diversified, loyal, crowded, rather independent community whose life centered around and was largely regulated by the church and its officers. Whether it occurred to the parishioners that they were living in one of the most stirring and colorful periods of English history we do not know. Probably they were more occupied with earning enough for food and shelter and clothing, with birth and marriage and families, with life and death. With some of this we shall also be concerned.

II: The Parish and the Records

The curate of St. Botolph's without Aldgate in 1558, when the clerk began the first record of burials in the parish, seems to have been one Richard Dabbes (Atkinson 1898). He was followed in 1564 by Robert Heaz, or Hayes[1] (18 June 1581), who served apparently until August 1587. Hayes died "of the gravell and the stone" and was buried on 6 April 1594. His successor was Christopher Therkill, or Threlkeld, who first read the lesson at St. Botolph's on Sunday afternoon, 20 August 1587. Some years later Mr. Threlkeld got into serious difficulties: "Our curatt was Excomunicated at whyt chaple on tuesday the 30th day of November Anno 1596 by m[r] Stephens the minister of Whyt Chaple." However, on 2 February 1596 Master Threl-

1. Elizabethan spelling, even of proper names, was cheerfully casual.

keld was "admitted agayne into the Ministrie." There is no explanation as to what happened, but the entry recording his burial a few months later, on 11 July 1597 (he died at the age of 53), seems to give a clue—"he dyed of inward griefe of mind or of a thowght." Elizabethan ideas about mental illness, including death supposedly from a "thought," or depression, will be discussed in a later chapter. In the case of the unfortunate Master Threlkeld, it seems possible that his temporary excommunication may have been caused by irrational behavior or statements that resulted from his illness.

Christopher Threlkeld was followed in 1597, according to Atkinson, by Paul Bush, or Bushey. He in turn was succeeded, apparently in December 1604, by Henry Rigges. The burials of three of his sons are recorded, Henry on Christmas Day 1605 (this in a note in the curate's own hand), Robert three months later, and James not long after that, on 8 April 1606. Such tragedies were not uncommon in those days of high infant and child mortality. Succeeding ministers of the parish, again according to Atkinson, were Edward Gadbold in 1608, William Biddulph in 1610, Robert Pritchett in 1611, John Brigges in 1611, and Samuel Bourman in 1625.

Other parish officials included the churchwardens, sidesmen (assistants to the churchwardens), overseers for the poor, sexton, and clerk (25 April 1617). Ward officials were the aldermen's deputies, counselors, members of the wardmote inquest, constables, beadles, scavengers, and rakers. They were elected at an assembly of the citizens of the ward called a wardmote (21 December 1593; 21 December 1595). The constable was an officer of the peace who carried out administrative duties and arrested vagrants. During a plague epidemic he was supposed to report the number of deaths and to quarantine buildings where there were plague victims. He might be assisted by the beadle (Wilson 1927). Scavengers and rakers collected and removed filth, garbage, and other debris from the streets.

Although the churchwardens were parish officials, they shared with the constables the responsibility for carrying out certain civil statutes, particularly those relating to the poor (Trotter 1919). The churchwardens also supervised the church building and property.

Periodically the parish had a "visitation" by the archdeacon or his representative. The visiting dignitary asked many questions which the churchwardens and sidesmen were sworn to answer (19 January 1590), listened to the presentments of offending parishioners, and inspected the church building and grounds. After the formalities ended, a banquet was given by the churchwardens. When Dr. Willens, the Archdeacon of London, made his visitation to St. Botolph's on 19 January 1590, the dinner "was kept at the signe of the St Jhons head in gratius Striette." Ten officials of the church—the former curate, the curate, the two churchwardens, the four sidesmen, the clerk, and the sexton—and their wives attended, as did seventeen "Bidden gesse [guests]" including four wives. Presumably the church officials and their ladies were included automatically while the remaining guests were specially invited. The "bidden" guests included "A butcher of S^t nycholas shambles [abattoir] and his man" and "Stephen an owld man that useth to go w^t Mr Threlkeld [the curate] and his wife." Finally, of course, there was the guest of honor.

It was a good dinner. The clerk set down the charges as follows:

Item a Ribb of Beefe at xvj^d		
the stone^2 and wayenge iiij stone	v^s	iiij^d
Item ij Lardge leggs of mutton at	iij^s	viij^d
Item ij capons at	iij^s	viij^d
Item j Breast of veale at		xx^d
Item j Loyne of veale at	ij^s	vj^d
Item in Bread		xviij^d
Item viij gallons of Beare and ale	ij^s	viij^d
Item in fyer [fuel for cooking]		vj^d
Item ij gallons of clarret wyne		
and 1 pottell [bottle] of whyt wyne	v^s	
Item for orrengis		ij^d
Item for Dressynge the meate		
and for plate & naperye	vj^s	
Some [sum]	xxxij^s	viij^d

Even for 38 guests there must have been almost enough of food and drink!

2. One stone equals 14 lb.

Announcements of the banns, or intent to marry, and weddings of course appear frequently in the records and are duly followed by notices of christenings and "churchings."[3] Most such entries are routine, but one unusual wedding is described in detail by John Clerke, clerk of the parish on 7 December 1618.

Thomas Speller a dumbe person by trade a Smith, of hatfield Broadoake in the Countie of Essex, and Sara Earle, daughter to John Earle of great Parington in the Countie aforesaid, were Maried by a Licence from Doctor Edwardes Chauncellor of the dioces of London: the seaventh day of December Anno Dm 1618. which Licence aforesaid was graunted at the request of Sir Francis Barrington knight and others of the place above-named, who by their Letters certified Mr Chauncellor, that the parents of either of them had given their consente to the said Mariage. And the said Thomas Speller the Dumbe partie, his willingnes to have the said Mariage rites solemmized, appeared, by bringing the Booke of Comon prayer (and his licence) in the one hand, and his Bride in the other unto the Minister of our parish Mr Briggs, and made the best signes he could, to show that he was willing to be maried, which was performed accordinglie, And also, the Lord Cheife Justice of the Kings Bench, (as Mr Briggs was informed) was made acquainted with the said Mariage before it was

3. Services of thanksgiving after childbirth.

> celebrated and allowed the same Mariage to be lawfull.
> I have sett downe the order of this
> Mariage at long, because wee
> never had the like.
> John Clerke

One reads between the lines the clerk's doubts as to whether such a marriage was proper. He makes it clear that higher authority had approved, thus removing the onus from the parish.

Restrictions on burials are revealed in a few cases.

> Elizabeth Crawford, a young Maid of the Minories-street, was buried the Eight day of December Anno Dni 1617 . . . in the old Church-yard[4] had the black cloth, there was no buriall service used because she was accompted [considered] to be a Recusant. She was buried in ye night.

Recusancy, that is, failure to attend services of the established church, was indirectly a serious charge, since a recusant at that period was automatically suspected of being a Catholic and therefore open to persecution. Surely it was an act of kindness that the body was decently laid to rest, even if the interment was done surreptitiously, at night, and in the old graveyard which was no longer used. It is interesting

4. A new burial ground had been opened on 18 April 1615 in Rosemarie Street in East-smithfield and had been consecrated by John, Bishop of London. Even the cemeteries were crowded. Rowse (1951) suggests that the scene in *Hamlet* in which the gravediggers find bones from an earlier burial was not an exaggeration.

that the clerk faithfully recorded this act of doubtful legality. Perhaps he decided that omitting this incident from his record would be even more serious. Again, on 18 August 1623 Anne Billings, a Dutch widow, was buried in the churchyard, but "there was no buriall service said at hir buriall, because she was reported to be a papist."

The body of a suicide could be denied interment in a churchyard. This issue came up on the death of "John Blackman, servant to Thomas Smedley Carman. he died of a wound which he gave him selfe in his sicknes being as it were distraught and light headed, and after the Coroners Enquest had viwed him, order was apointed to have him laid in Christian buriall. y^t seemed he was ill lookt unto in his sicknes" (10 July 1624). This means that an inquest was held on a technical suicide. It was then decided that because the sick man could not be held responsible for taking his life while irrational and neglected by his attendant —if he had one—his body should not be denied the last rites.

Next to the minister, the clerk was the most important parish official. By the sixteenth century his major function was to keep the parish accounts and records. We shall see much evidence that the clerks of St. Botolph's were meticulous. By necessity, they were also remarkably well informed about what went on, officially and unofficially, properly and improperly, in the parish. Since their record was accessible to the minister and others and was on occasion inspected by outside authorities, the clerks were obliged to be cautious about their statements but at the same time not to shun unpleasant truths. Thus we read, for example, of the burial of a sailor, long sick, who lived in the house of Joan Blonn-stone, a widow. She "kept him at her howse and said he was her husband, but I have heard sence, it was not trewe" (11 October 1595).

The almost omniscient clerks did not hesitate to record illegitimacy, and could and did name the father as well as the mother. The occasion was usually the burial record of an infant dead at birth or soon afterward.

A woman chylde the daughter of Isbell Hardinge a single woman, Being a miss woman[5] who some tyme dwelt with Nicolas Boren a victuler[6] in swan alye being in the libertie of East Smithfield. The sayde woman was brought a bed or delivered of the sayde childe in the striete . . . and the chylde Being brought to the howse of Robert Mott a sayler dwellinge in the waye as we go toward the Mineries [Minories] . . . it was by the consent of Richard casye the aldermans deputie and Robert prieste the con-stable Buried by Lawrence ponder the sexton the xxii[nd] Daye of June in ano 1587 beinge stillborne.

A woman chyld the reputed daughter to Abraham Duke servant to Thomas Norton a gardener being begotten of

5. Mistress or, less commonly, a prostitute.
6. Innkeeper.

the boddie of Jeane Tunkins a single woman late servant to Thomas Anvell a carpenter. wch said Jeane Tunkins was delivered of the said chyld in the cage[7] near whyt chapel barres, where the said [child] Dyed not being christned and was buried the xxiiij Day of April Anno 1599.

Edward Sendall, a Bastard, sonne to one Edward Sendall of hemnell in Norfolk, begotten of one Margery Spall delivered of it in this parish. [5 January 1611]

Abraham Haddocke the reputed sonne of Israel Haddock, a Towle-taker [toll collector] in harrow Alley, the mother named [blank space] a single woman who was delivered in the street, and like a Base Strumpet kame away and left hir child behinde hir, which was Christned the fift day of Febrary Anno Dni 1616, and the father of this Child also, who hath an honest wife of his owne, is runne away from hir, like a base varlet.

A marginal notation adds, "God send the Child more grace, then [sic] the wicked Parents."

James Dabbs, the reputed sonne of one Robert Dabbs a Maried man (and at this time in Newgate [prison] the mother named hester Warner a single-woman & a strumpet, and was delivered of Child in the house of widow Schetchley of Rosemarie lane. . . .) [19 September 1618]

7. A kind of very small jail for petty criminals.

Many more entries of this nature appear. The record book also shows the burial of a woman who died in the house of one widow Russell in Rosemarie Lane, "a Comon harbourer of Strange Ghests [guests] to Charge the parish." In other words, the clerk knew very well about the dubious characters who lived at the widow's house and received charity from the parish.

The first clerk of St. Botolph's to be identified by name was Christopher Cork, who served from July 1564 to October 1580. A respected parishioner, "always off good name & fame deceassed in the feare of god, he was buried in the church" (6 October 1580).[8] He evidently had an immediate successor; at least there is no break in the record.

The appointment of the next clerk, Thomas Harrydance, apparently began in January 1582. His name appears occasionally in the records—"I Thomas Harrydance the wrighter heareof being the parish clarke" (8 October 1594)—but we learn little more about him until we come to the notation of his burial.

Thomas Harridance Cittizen and Iron-monger of London, and Parish Clarke here in this parish for the space of Nineteen yeares and five Monethes, was buried the Nineteenth day of June, Anno Domini 1601. he was a verie Carefull and Industrious man in his place.

8. Because London graveyards were crowded, many additional bodies were buried under the stones of the church floor.

An individual named John Maddreyne is mentioned on 17 June 1602 as being the clerk, but I have found no indication of how long he served.

By January 1616 one John Clerke was parish clerk (6 September 1618). He was a girdler, or girdle maker. The fact that both John Clerke and Thomas Harrydance were tradesmen, the latter being an ironmonger (see above), makes it clear that the clerk's position was only a part-time occupation. There is intermittent mention of Clerke through 1620. On 6 September 1621 it is noted that

> there was a Quarterlie Sermon made in our Church, for the Comemoration of Mrs. Anne Clarke widow late of hounsditch Deceased, and ten Dozen of Bread given the poore of the parish, five shillings to the Minister for the Sermon, and xij^d to the Clarke and Sextons for their Attendance, which Order is to be observed four tymes in the yeare for ever according to a vestrey decree made for that purpose.

> This Charge was defray'd by me John Clerke,
> hir late Brother-in-law.

The record shows that the prescribed service and distribution of gifts paid for by Clerke took place again on 6 September 1622, 7 September 1623, 5 September 1624, and 12 December 1624.

John Clerke probably died in the terrible plague epidemic

of the summer of 1625, for the beautifully clear lettering in which he entered his notations ends abruptly and without explanation on 5 July of that year, to be replaced with a hasty and different hand. He must have been a man of substance and a prominent member of the parish. Such a status would help to explain the biting comments about foolish or unpopular or sinning parishioners that characterize his notations. On weddings:

> William Ley, and Jane Arrooes widow, and a Notorius Scould, of Swan alley, were married the tenth day of August Anno Dni 1617. this is hir 4th husband.

> John Collier a Musition of Beare-Alley in the high-street, who had Continewed a heavie widower the space of three whole weekes; did cheare uppe his spirite again, and was Maried to one Agnes Swayne a widow his neere Neighbour, on Sunday the xxviij[th] day of December Anno Dni 1617.
>
> he would have bene maried soonener, but that he was loth to be at the charg of a license.

The musician did not survive very long[9] to enjoy whatever bliss befell him, for on 27 May 1621

> Richard Batcheller waterman of S[t] Saviours parish in Southwarke, & Agnes Collier widow of our parish, were Married. . . .

9. His burial is not recorded in the parish. Presumably he died elsewhere.

Shee was late wife of John Collier Musition, late of our parish.

Two beggars who were married 17 February 1617 were unkindly dismissed as "both of the Scumm of our parish."

Robert Dearelove, Nayle-maker, and Jane Snow (a froward[10] widow) of Rosemarie lane, were married (with much a doe). [25 May 1618]

One couple did not pay the marriage fee, and Clerke notes disgustedly, "wee had for this wedding Nihil in a Bagg" (25 April 1619).

William Dennis a Porter and Joane Wellar, both of our parish, were Maried. . . . shee was servant to one Richard Tiptoe of our parish as honest a man as is in the cards when ye kinge be out. The Bride was a peece of Crackt Stuff. [1 September 1619]

Thomas Grove Waterbearer, and Katherine King widow, both of our parish were Maried. . . . The said Thomas Grove continued a widower almost vj weekes. [3 December 1620]

Of the wedding of a thread maker to the daughter of a porter:

The man was about xvij yeares of Age and ye woman xiiij.

10. Refractory, ungovernable.

A worthie Ancient Couple of young Fooles. [6 July 1623]

William Clare Gunn-smith, and Marie Scarlett widow, were Maried . . . shee was late wife to one John Scarlett victualler of our parish.

> And continewed a widow ten weekes.
> [27 November 1623]

A few of the numerous christenings also stirred the clerk's ire. To the record of one such event on 27 November 1618, he added sourly, "The Couple were maried 7 weeks & 3 days before this Christning." Another entry for a christening has the comment "were maried about xxij Dayes before" (18 March 1624). Even the dead did not always escape.

Goodleffe Scraggs wife to James Scraggs Cutler, who dwelt neere unto the Tower ditch,[11] in the libertie of Eastsmithfield was buried. . . .

> She was a woman of Antiquitie:
> and kept a house of Iniquitie. [14 October 1621]

Christian Whaller a widow, who dwelt in east Smithfield, was buried the xxiiij[th] day of Julie Anno Dni 1622. Shee was coffind in the New Church-yard, and had the Blacke cloth, but nothing paid for hir buriall.

She used much, to goe to law
and prov'd hir selfe a verie daw,[12]   } These are the fruites
and dyed upon a pad of straw.   of Idle Suites.

11. The moat around the Tower of London.
12. A jackdaw, a bird similar to a crow.

But the clerk had a kind word for the good.

> Ezechias le Roy Hemp-dresser, who dwelt in minories
> street . . . was buried in the Chauncell, and had a knell
> with the great Bell. there was xxx^{tie} dozen of Bread dis-
> tributed amongst the poore, the same day.
>
> The poore lost a good friend and the parish a good
> Neighbour. [20 December 1620]

Obviously the records were of importance to the parish
itself, but there was a more fundamental reason why banns,
weddings, christenings, and burials were carefully and regularly set down. Parish records were not known in England
before the reign of Henry VIII, although, as Burn (1862)
points out, "marriages and Burials were recorded in *Churches*
long before the 16th century, not indeed in a Register
specially provided for the purpose, but in the Missals and
Psalters in use in the Church." The introduction of parish
records was due to Thomas Cromwell, Vicar General and
Advisor to Henry, who on 5 September 1538 issued an important decree (Birch 1759; Waters 1887).

> *Item;* That you, and every parson, vicar, or curate within
> this diocess, shall for every church keep one book or
> register, wherein he shall write the day and year of every
> wedding, christning, and burying, made within your parish
> for your time, and so every man succeeding you likewise;
> and also there insert every person's name that shall be so
> wedded, christned, and buried; and for the safe keeping
> of the same book, the parish shall be bound to provide,

of their common charges, one sure coffer with two locks
and keys, whereof the one to remain with you, and the
other with the church wardens of every such parish
wherein the said book shall be laid up; which book ye
shall every Sunday take forth, and in the presence of the
said wardens, or one of them, write and record in the
same, all the weddings, christnings, and buryings, made
the whole week afore; and that done, to lay up the book
in the said coffer, as afore: and for every time that the
same shall be omitted, the party that shall be in the fault
thereof, shall forfeit to the said church 3s. 4d. to be employed in the reparation of the said church.[13]

The order was promptly and widely resented on the
ground that the information in the registers might be used
as a basis for new taxes. Of course this was not the idea, but
nevertheless there were open complaints, even though
Henry's savage laws threatened any critic of the government with prosecution for high treason. New mandates
almost identical with that of 1538 were issued in 1547,
1555, and in the early years of the reign of Elizabeth, and
inquiries regarding the proper keeping of the registers were
made at the annual visitations to the parishes (Cox 1910).

In 1563 and again in 1590 Parliament attempted to force
the bishops and archbishops to set up a center in each diocese
where transcripts of every parish register would be kept.
The costs, which no doubt would have been considerable,

13. The spelling has been modernized by Burnet (1829), in
whose book the text appears.

were to be paid from special fees charged at every wedding, christening, and burial (Cox 1910; Tate 1951). However, this measure was strongly opposed by the Church and was defeated.

On 25 October 1597 the clergy of Canterbury passed a provincial constitution obliging each parish to keep careful records in a book of parchment, paid for by the parish. Into this were to be copied the old paper registers. Their importance was emphasized. The Queen gave her approval in 1598 to this measure.[14] The constitution also directed that each Sunday at the end of a service all new entries in the register were to be read to the congregation—this to prevent omissions or inaccurate notations—and that every page was to bear the names of the churchwardens and minister (Cox 1910). The mandate specified that the old registers were to be transcribed from their earliest dates "but especially since the first year of her Majesty's reign," i.e., 1558. It is believed that this is why many parchment transcriptions started with this year rather than 1538, when the paper registers were undertaken at Cromwell's direction (Rowse 1951; Tate 1951). It will be recalled that the parish records of St. Botolph began in 1558.

In 1603 the Church issued another order which in general reiterated that of 1597. It was specified that the parchment be stored in a chest with three locks, the keys to which were to be kept by the minister and churchwardens (Cox 1910).

14. Cox 1910; Tate 1951; Waters 1887.

There are twelve volumes of record books from the
Parish of St. Botolph without Aldgate that I used for my
study. The books vary in size, some being quite large. The
period I investigated was from 1558, when the record books
and the reign of Elizabeth began, to 1625, when James's
reign ended. Several of the volumes overlap in terms of
dates, and given volumes may have omissions, but taken as
a whole the record is nearly complete. Almost all of the
pages are in at least reasonably good condition and are
legible.

The pages in the books designated MSS. 9221 and 9234/1
through 9234/7 are of paper and are written in different
hands. These almost certainly are the original records rather
than transcripts. The other volumes, MSS. 9220, 9222/1,
9223, and 9234/8, have parchment pages. MSS. 9221 and
9234/1–7 are for the period 1570–98, that is, they were
written in or before the year when Elizabeth approved the
provincial constitution of 1597 requiring parchment record
books. The remaining four volumes are all transcripts.

MS. 9221 was written by Robert Hayes, curate of the
parish from 1564 until probably 1587. It covers the period
from 1570 until 1593, indicating that Master Hayes continued his clerical duties after his retirement. The years
1570–93 are covered with extensive overlapping by MSS.
9222/1 and 9234/1. The latter begins:

Heare after is speacefyed and then regestred all suche
things as is done in ye churche the tyme that henry ponder
is ye church warden of ye parish church of sent Buttolphs

withoute Allgate beginenge the 15th daye of Desember in ano 1583.

The clerk's name is not given.

An entry in MS. 9234/4 for 31 May 1594 lists the church members present at a vestry meeting and continues:

Item at the fore said vestrie howlden in the parish church . . . of St Buttolphes without Aldgate london . . . it was agreed that Thomas Harrydance being the parish clarke shall have the keping and entring of the Regester belonging to the said parish church for Christnings Wedings and burialls. And that he shalbe alowed for entring of the same, owt of the church wardens accompte the yearly stypent of fortie shillings by the yeare and his quarter to be due unto him at Midsomer[15] next at which tyme he is to receyve the some of tenn shillings and so forthe he is to receyve it quarterlie.

This volume is in the hand of Master Harrydance.

For 17 October 1594 of the same volume there is a

Memerandum that Thomas harrydance our parishe Clarke being warned by Richard Goodman a clarke belonging to Mr Blackwells office to bring the church Regester . . . to Mr Doctor Stanhop to his chamber being in the Doctors comons[16] . . . the said parish clarke did carrie the said

15. Midsummer Day, 24 June; one of the quarter days.
16. Doctors' Commons, an organization of ecclesiastical lawyers, occupied houses near St. Paul's Cathedral. See page 18 for earlier reference to Doctor Stanhope.

regester to him the foresaid day at whych tyme Mr Doctor Stanhop willed our said parish clarke to leave the same there with him who was to peruse the same as he said for some matter which did conserne himselfe.

Doctor Stanhope returned the record book to the clerk on 25 October. Presumably it had an official inspection first.

Master Harrydance indicates again on 9 June 1596 that he is keeping the record book. On 5 October 1597 he notes:

Heare in this Booke conteyned 5 quires[17] of Paper which did Cost me 8 d the quyre	iij^s iiij^d
payd more for halfe a velme [vellum] of parchment to bynd the same in	vj^d
payd for bynding of the same	vj^d

Some iiij^s iiij^d besyde that
I spent in fetching of same xxj^d

On 17 October 1599, the year after Elizabeth's mandate about parish record books, the churchwardens got around to taking action and

did by the consent of the rest of the parishioners and vestrie men Bye a newe booke of parchament for the behalfe of the churche to Regester All Christnings, weddings, and burialls in, sence the tyme of the beginning of the Queenes Majesties Raigne.

17. A quire originally was four sheets of paper folded into eight leaves. Later it came to mean 24 sheets. Since this volume (MS. 9234/6) has about 300 large leaves, it contains more than five quires.

The new book cost five pounds. The next day the new

> regester of parchement was delivered . . . to Thomas
> Abott a scrivener dwelling in the libertie of Eastsmith-
> field, by whome all christnings, wedings & burialls are to
> be written into the same by the derection of Mr Nycholas
> Reynolds [a vestryman] et c.

The old register was also sent to Master Reynolds with
word that

> dyvers leaves thereof weare Loose, and to deliver the said
> booke to Thomas Abbott to be entered into the foresaid
> new Regester according to order.

On 30 October the old register now repaired and "with a
red Leather cover and a buckle was delivered to Thomas
Abbott" for copying. Still later

> I did deliver unto Thomas Abott the church Regester
> with the black leather cover being the last book that was
> made for the parish of paper in Mr Hayze [the curate]
> his time. [26 November]

This must have been what is now MS. 9221. On 13 December 1599 the vestry authorized payment of £6 13s. 4d. to
Thomas Abbott for his transcriptions, not yet complete.
Henry Riggs, the curate, began keeping the register at the
end of December 1604, but how long he continued is not
stated.

MS. 9223 lists all the christenings from October 1593 to 29 March 1607.

Begon by Robert Heaz sometime Curate of the said Parish, and Thomas Harrydance then Parish Clarke there, the rest was copied out of the great Register Booke belonging to the said Parish, and finished in Moneth of October, Anno Domini 1618, By me John Clerke Girdler (at that time the Parish Clarke there).

Soli Deo, laus, Honor et Gloria. Amen.

MS. 9223 also lists the burials from 1 October 1593 to the end of November 1618. Again the records begun by Hayes and Harridance were copied and continued by Clerke.

One reason that parish registers are important is that they provided the source material for what came to be known as bills of mortality. These were periodic lists of the deaths, and later also of the births, for a given area, usually a parish, or for a series of parishes. Angus (1854) felt that "to the plague the public of London owed their bills of christenings and burials," but he erred in believing that the bills were not begun until 1592. There is mention of a bill of mortality in London as early as 30 August 1519, when the Court of Aldermen ordered payment for a list of deaths (Wilson 1927). Brett-James (1935) mentions the existence of weekly bills for August of 1527 and 1528. A letter dated October 1532 refers to such a list; according to Wilson (1927), who has reviewed the development of the bills, the data for this list presumably were collected by special surveys. Wilson states that by 1536, a plague year, the parish clerks of London were under instructions to supply written lists weekly of the names of the sick and deceased to the Lord Mayor.

The British Museum is reported to have a bill of mortality (MS. Egerton 2603, fol. 4) dating from November 1532[18] or possibly from as early as 1512 (Creighton 1902; Wilson 1927). The only cause of death given on the bill is plague. Other weekly bills from before 1600 that are reported to exist are two for 5–14 August 1535,[19] one for 16–22 November 1582,[20] and one for 28 December 1581–17 December 1582.[21] The last bill is said to list christenings, total deaths, and plague deaths by parishes for the City of London and liberties.

In 1545–46 an agreement was reached between the Lord Mayor of London and the Parish Clerks' Company[22] to the

18. Brett-James 1935; Kargon 1963; Mullett 1956.

19. *State Papers, Henry VIII*, par. 49, fols. 219–26 (Brett-James 1935; Wilson 1927).

20. Hist. MSS. Comm., Salisbury MSS., pt. xiii, p. 212 (Brett-James 1935; Wilson 1927). These two authorities also list surviving seventeenth-century bills.

21. Brett-James 1935; Ditchfield 1907; Walford 1878.

22. The parish clerks were originally incorporated in London in 1233 as the Clerks of St. Nicholas, and their original concern was with church music. They also gave plays. Only later did the collection and recording of information become their responsibility (Creighton 1891; Wilson 1927). "It was the singular history of a Company which gained its greatest name as the Registrars of Births and Deaths in London down to the Registration Act of 1837, to have

effect that the latter would notify the common crier of "the
name and surname of any freeman that shall die having any
children under the age of 21 years" (Ditchfield 1907). Bills
were kept for a few weeks in 1551 during an epidemic of
of "sweating sickness" (Creighton 1891). Weekly returns
to the Lord Mayor from every parish giving the numbers
of plague deaths and total deaths were required in London
by 1553 (Christie 1893; Wilson 1927). Two years later it
was directed that the parish clerks report "the numbers of
all the persons that do die and whereof they die," but the
reports continued to identify only plague as a cause of death
(Wilson 1927).

The earliest *printed yearly* bill of mortality seems to have
been for 1563, but it is reported to be lost (Brett-James
1935). *Weekly* bills, begun on 21 December 1592 (Birch
1759), may have first been printed in 1593 (Wilson 1927),
but probably did not begin to appear regularly until the end
of 1603.[23] The earliest *surviving* printed weekly bill, pre-
served in the Guildhall Library (Broadsides 6.99), is for the
week beginning 13 October 1603. Bills were on sale to the
public at 4s. yearly in 1594 (Walford 1878). The oldest
surviving printed yearly bill gives data for 1603 and 1625;
it was printed in the latter year. The Company of Parish
Clerks took over the printing of the bills in 1626. There was

---

been not only the first Choral Society but also the first company of
stage players" (Creighton 1891).
23. Birch 1759; Brett-James 1935; Graunt 1759.

a severe penalty for premature disclosure of their contents to the public (Wilson 1927).

Against this historical background, one may appreciate that the records of the Parish of St. Botolph without Aldgate are in several respects very unusual if not unique. They have not previously been analyzed; Atkinson's history of the parish (1898) quotes briefly from them but does not undertake their review. Unlike many parish registers, they appear never to have been published (Cox 1910), and hence have been available only in the original manuscript volumes. The usual register simply lists baptisms, weddings, and burials with the names of the persons involved and in most cases the dates. Age, occupation, and supposed cause of death are seldom indicated (Eversley 1966). On the other hand, the St. Botolph records are remarkably detailed and really constitute a kind of daybook, as has already in part been indicated. The "causes" of death are reported (see chap. 4). The circumstances of violent and accidental deaths are outlined, sometimes with particulars (see chap. 6).

The relative antiquity of the record books of St. Botolph's Church is not exceptional. Wrigley (1966) states, "A few hundred English registers go right back to 1538 and a much larger number is still extant from the early seventeenth century." It is much less common for the record of christenings and burials to begin early and continue without interruption.[24] The St. Botolph record of these events is unbroken

24. The Parish of Colyton, Devon, is very unusual in having a continuous register of christenings, marriages, and burials from 1538 to 1837 (Wrigley 1966).

from 1558 to 1625, the arbitrary stopping point for this study, and beyond. John Graunt in the seventeenth century published continuous annual totals for christenings and burials for the country parishes of Tiverton in Devonshire from 1560 to 1664, of Cranbrook in Kent from 1560 to 1649, and of "that in Hantshire" for 1569 to 1658. His regular and continuous data for London as a whole or for its parishes individually do not begin until 18 December 1623 (Graunt 1759).

The "cause" of death became part of the burial record at St. Botolph's in 1583 but, except for "plague," seems not to have been recorded on the bills of mortality or elsewhere for London, or for parishes or towns outside it, until 1607 (Wilson 1927). The practice was subsequently abandoned until 1624.[25] Christie (1893) says that for Westminster and the outparishes of the City of London, cause of death was simply noted on a plague or no-plague basis until as late as approximately 1660. Thus the St. Botolph records for 1583 to 1599 of "causes" of death appear to be unique for the sixteenth century.

Age at death is important information; beginning in 1583 it was recorded by the clerk of St. Botolph. This practice also was apparently most unusual at that time. Wrigley

25. According to other authorities, recording of the supposed cause of death was not begun until 1629 (Brett-James 1935) or 1632 (Graunt 1759), but these later dates may simply mark resumptions of the practice.

(1966) finds it "very remarkable that an exact age at burial" is included from 1571 to 1586 in the register book of St. Michael le Belfrey, York, and he indicates further (1968) that it was exceptional until 1813 for parish registers to report age at death. The St. Botolph records are particularly valuable because "cause" of death and age can be correlated.

Says Graunt (1759), "It may now be asked, to what purpose tends all this laborious bustling and groping to know? . . ." To this very reasonable question the ensuing chapters will be addressed.

III: Births and Deaths

The founder of the science of vital statistics was a Londoner, John Graunt (1620–74). Haberdasher and freeman of the Drapers' Company, he seems to have become interested in public affairs through his activities in his ward, where he held several political offices, and then as a member of the Common Council of the City of London. In addition, he served as captain and later as major in the trained band, a kind of militia. His *Natural and Political Observations on the Bills of Mortality* was first published in 1662, utilizing data from the bills for a period beginning with the end of 1603. The bills, which had appeared only sporadically for some years before then, were resumed in 1603 because of an outbreak of plague (Angus 1854).

Counting the population was not new in the sixteenth and seventeenth centuries. Censuses were taken in Roman times and no doubt earlier, and estimates of the numbers of individuals being born or dying must also have been made on occasion. Part of the impetus for such counts in England can be traced back to Cromwell's injunction of 1538, and more of it came from the necessity for counting dead during plague epidemics. But there were no English censuses until much later. Graunt's contribution was to compile and interpret available information, particularly from the bills of mortality. He was the first to show that more boys are born than girls, the sex ratio from his data for 1628 to 1662 being 110.0 males to 100 females at birth and 106.8:100 at death. He philosophizes:

> So that although more men die violent deaths than women, that is, more are slain in wars, killed by mischance, drowned at sea, and die by the hand of justice; moreover, more men go to colonies, and travel into foreign parts, than women; and lastly, more remain unmarried than of women, as fellows of colleges, and apprentices above eighteen, & c. yet the said thirteenth part difference [106.8:100] bringeth the business but to such a pass, that every woman may have a husband, without the allowance of polygamy. . . . more males being born than females, more also die. [1759]

Graunt demonstrated that country people were more

healthy than city people and estimated the total population
after determining the death rate. His research helped to win
him such distinction that, although he was a tradesman, he
was elected one of the first Fellows of the recently founded
Royal Society of London. This was at the specific direction of
Charles II, who told that already prestigious body "that if
they found any more such tradesmen, they should be sure to
admit them all, without anymore adoe."[1]

Graunt recognized that parish registers and the information compiled from them may contain serious errors, an ob-
servation since confirmed by historical demographers. Let
us examine the extent to which some sources of error suggested by specialists for parish registers may apply to the St.
Botolph record books.

First is the possibility of negligence or carelessness on the
part of the clerk or curate who made the entires, as pointed
out by Hollingsworth (1968). Like the suspicion of coward-
ice or infidelity, the accusation of error is usually much easier
to raise than to disprove. However, Wilson's study (1927) of
burial records in London parishes in the early seventeenth
century reveals an overall discrepancy between those records
and the deaths reported in the bills of mortality of less than
1 percent. Plague deaths were an exception, being often un-
derreported. The possibility of significant mistakes made by
those who kept the records at St. Botolph's cannot be denied,

1. Cooper 1908; Garrison 1929; Glass 1963; Singer and Underwood 1962.

but it seems unlikely. Both the edict of 1538 and later regulations required weekly inspection of the books by the churchwardens and periodic examinations by diocesan officers. My reading of the books, particularly those kept or copied by Robert Hayes, Thomas Harrydance, and John Clerke, yielded a strong subjective impression of meticulous care.

An internal check on a sizable sample of the St. Botolph data is provided by the count kept by Hayes, a curate, of the burials he performed. It may be recalled that Hayes served from 1564 to 1587 and that his clerk from 1564 to 1580 was one Christopher Cork. On 18 June 1581 the record states:

> Here it is to be noted that I Robart Heaz curat of this church under hir m^{aty} beganne in my service the 14 of July anno 1564 from the wch tyme & daye until the 18 of this present June Anno 1581 I have buryed 2722.

My count of burials for the same period is 2,699, a discrepancy of 0.84 percent. The record for 21 November 1582 says:

> Here is to be noted that I Robert Heaz curat of this church under her Matie from the iv. of June 1581 until the 21 of November [1582] have buried 366 so that in the hole [whole] from the 14 of July 1564 untill the foresaid Daie of Noveb^{er} 1582 [I have buried a total of] 3088.

My own count, adjusted for the fact that I kept monthly totals for the period 4 June 1581 to 21 November 1582, is 368.

It should be added that we do not know the name of the clerk who presumably succeeded Cork in 1580 and preceded Thomas Harrydance, whose appointment began in January 1582. (Remember that the new year began 25 March and that January 1582 was after November 1582). It is possible that Hayes himself served as clerk in the interim; if so, his count for that period would be based on his own record and would not then provide a test of his care. In any case, such evidence as we have seems to be all in favor of accuracy on the part of the clerk.

Birch (1759) was concerned with errors arising from the undoubted fact that some people born in one parish died in another parish in London or in the country. Graunt (1759) proved that large numbers of people migrated from the country into London; my findings agree. It should also be emphasized that in my own tabulations there is no attempt to segregate nonparishioners from those who belonged to the Parish of St. Botolph without Aldgate, primarily because the migrant portion of the population in London, and in other English towns, between 1558 and 1625 was very large (see chap. 7). One should rather regard my monthly and yearly counts as samplings on a parish-wide basis of that impoverished, badly housed, sometimes malnourished, and occasionally migratory group that constituted a large segment of London's population.

The question arises as to what percentage of the babies born in the parish were baptized there. This is an important point, since the records show, with a few exceptions, not births but christenings. There were several reasons why an infant might not be baptized. One was that a few stillborn infants did not receive this rite; however, these and other stillborns were identified as such in the records of St. Botolph's Parish. Also, parents might not seek baptism for their child, perhaps because they were dissenters or Roman Catholics and did not accept the Church of England service. This possibility was regarded by several critics[2] as a source of considerable error in estimating numbers of births, but all of them were speaking of a period after 1650. Earlier, during the reigns of Elizabeth and James, it was dangerous to be known in London as a Catholic or as a noncommunicant of the Church of England. Not to attend services regularly and not to subscribe to the forms of the Church—baptism, marriage, burial—was to make one immediately and obviously suspect as a papist and thus to invite serious trouble.[3]

Graunt (1759) was concerned about "the scruples, which many public ministers would make of the worthiness of parents to have their children baptized." He felt that such objections would prevent baptisms and thus cause births to go unrecorded. There is no way to prove that the ministers of St. Botolph's may not on occasion have denied baptism to a child because the parents were considered unworthy. But the frequent references in the record books to unsavory in-

2. Angus 1854; Birch 1759; Eversley 1966; Graunt 1759.
3. Brinkworth 1942; Lunt 1957; Rowse 1951.

dividuals to whom, or to whose children, the rites of the church were nevertheless granted (chap. 2) make it seem unlikely that the ministers allowed prejudice to rule. Similarly it has been suggested that unwillingness or inability to pay the small baptismal fee resulted in numerous unchristened, and hence uncounted, children (Angus 1854; Graunt 1759). One can only answer that the clerks occasionally indicate that no fee was received for a christening performed (entries for 6 September 1590, 27 June 1591, and many others). Indeed it appears that for a time toward the end of the century no fees were collected from anyone for baptisms.

Similar criticisms are heard when it is debated whether the numbers of burials indicate the true numbers of deaths. Birch (1759) and Angus (1854) both feared that only members of the Church of England would be buried according to its rites. But, as in the case of the christenings, the religious argument is unconvincing. More important, the law required that the clerk be notified of all deaths in the parish, and the parish was obliged to bury its dead unless it succeeded in the difficult task of persuading another parish to do so. Hollingsworth (1968) suggests that a mortality rate of 200 to 250 deaths per thousand infants in the first year of life was to be expected and that figures yielding lower death rates are suspect. It will be shown later that the mortality rates for the first year of life based on the St. Botolph data are much higher than 250 per thousand.

Let us now turn to the record of christenings in St. Botolph's Parish. I counted these month by month from November 1558 through December 1626. The annual totals are shown in table 1. All of the totals unless otherwise specified will be for a *modern* calendar year, January through December.

Table 1. *Christenings (C) and Burials (B), 1558–1626*

Year	C	B
1558	(16)[a]	(44)[a]
1559	75	190
1560	93	119
1561	120	106
1562	102	105
1563	91	629
1564	87	68
1565	92	89
1566	82	83
1567	103	69
1568	103	103
1569	87	156
1570	97	285
1571	104	166
1572	108	124
1573	108	159
1574	94	237
1575	133	186
1576	145	147
1577	126	230
1578	153	327
1579	140	129
1580	157	129
1581	137	177
1582	173	304

a. Incomplete year.

Year	C	B
1583	165	281
1584	161	174
1585	185	160
1586	168	189
1587	168	298
1588	176	210
1589	226	256
1590	223	202
1591	193	215
1592	184	382
1593	171	1,463
1594	237	224
1595	204	175
1596	183	234
1597	195	358
1598	176	229
1599	221	259
1600	242	206
1601	202	222
1602	216	285
1603	232	1,948
1604	254	202
1605	250	263
1606	281	369
1607	291	350
1608	270	446
1609	269	477
1610	277	418
1611	291	355
1612	296	394
1613	274	317
1614	292	307
1615	295	363
1616	264	285
1617	272	359
1618	301	379
1619	331	318
1620	332	322

Year	C	B
1621	305	378
1622	330	403
1623	283	461
1624	302	505
1625	250	2,479
1626	263	250
Totals for period:	13,427	22,731

Total annual christenings and burials are shown graphically in figure 3. A fairly steady increase in christenings is evident.

One has the impression that it was the practice to baptize an infant soon after birth. Indeed, an exception on 11 October 1616 merited a special marginal notation: "This Child was a Moneth old, when it was Christned." Prompt baptism was encouraged by the precarious hold on life of some babies; many a child was given the rite at home "because it was weak" (see below). One study of data for the city of York in England between 1538 and 1750 involved both birth dates and baptismal dates for a limited number of infants; the author concluded that the average interval between the two events was approximately three days (Cowgill 1966). However, the St. Botolph record books almost never supply age at baptism, and it is possible that the ceremony sometimes was appreciably delayed, a source of error of which Eversley (1966) warns.

The records permit counts of "still-born" infants over fairly extended periods. We do not know exactly how the

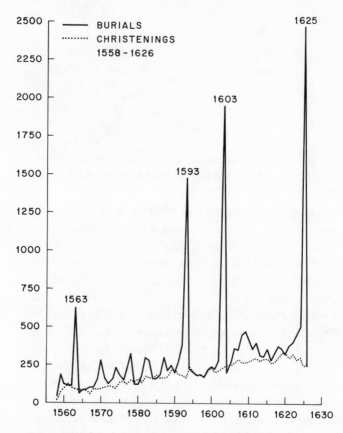

Fig. 3. Burials and christenings, 1558–1626. There were plague epidemics in 1563, 1593, 1603, and 1625. Note that in a given year burials usually exceeded christenings.

clerk would have defined *stillborn.* It is likely that he was talking about what we would call *fetal deaths,* that is, fetuses dying at any time during pregnancy as well as at term. The data must be regarded with some caution, since a very few entries indicate that an infant categorized as "stillborn" actually lived briefly after birth. For example, a child

> dyed and was buried the ixth day of May Anno 1596. which chyld was borne alyve the day before and for that he was not cristned he was accompted as stilborne.

A second infant died when

> abowt some seven dayes owld, not being cristned was buried the xvijth day of August anno 1596 wherefore accompted as stilbourne.

Two other similar cases are cited (19 July 1598; 24 November 1598). It appears that a conscientious clerk, feeling that every burial must be explained and lacking a category for babies born alive but dying before baptism, arbitrarily assigned these unfortunates to the "stillborn" group. Wrigley (1968) points out that the demographer must not count stillborn children baptized by the midwife as dying in the first month of life simply because they are reported as baptized. Such clerical reporting could indeed introduce error, but I have not found instances of it in the St. Botolph records. The midwife was enjoined to baptize an infant if it were likely not to survive and a clergyman was not at hand (Forbes

1966). She may on occasion have christened a stillborn baby. However, the necessity that she act because a minister could not arrive in time was much more likely to arise in rural areas than in a city parish.

Stillbirths for two periods, 1584–98 and 1609–23, are summarized in table 2.

If all stillbirths were correctly reported, the drop in the death rate for the second period as compared to the first, 124.2 to 44.6, is as impressive as it is mystifying. The plague epidemic in 1592 and 1593 is reflected in an increased rate of stillbirths. It appears, incidentally, that stillbirths were seldom recorded in other parishes (Eversley 1966).

By comparison, Graunt (1759) noted that

> the abortives and stillborn[4] are about the twentieth part [50 per 1000] of those, that are christned; and the numbers seemed the same thirty years ago [in 1632] as now, which shows there were more in proportion in those years than now; or else, that in these latter years due accounts have not been kept of the abortives, as having been buried without notice, and perhaps not in church-yards.

Graunt's stillbirth rate is within the range of those in table 2.

Official U.S. statistics for 1963 for "all fetal deaths regardless of period of gestation," that is, for fetuses dead during

4. The distinction is between fetuses born dead before the end of pregnancy and those delivered dead at term.

Table 2. Christenings, Burials of Stillborns, Chrisoms, and Infants, and Death Rate per 1000 Christenings, 1584–98 and 1609–23

5-year period	Christenings	Stillborn			Chrisoms	Infants	Death Rate per 1000 Christenings		
		Male	Female	Total			Stillborn	Chrisoms	Infants
1584–88	858	50	56	106	137	254	123.5	159.7	296.0
1589–93	997	74	59	133	175	348	133.4	175.5	349.0
1594–98	995	55	60	105	150	271	105.5	150.7	272.3
Subtotal	2,850	179	175	354	462	873	124.2	162.1	306.3
1609–13	1,961	58	42	100			51.0		
1614–18	1,693	43	26	69			40.8		
1619–23	1,882	53	25	78			41.4		
Subtotal	5,536	154	93	274			44.6		
Total	8,386	333	268	601			71.6		

pregnancy as well as at term, show an overall, combined rate for whites and nonwhites of 23.0 per 1,000 live births. In 1937 the comparable figure was 33.4 (Anon. 1965; Potter and Adair 1940). These figures are very much lower than the stillbirth rates in table 2, a circumstance that certainly does not argue per se for incomplete reporting by the clerks, although it does illustrate the fact that fetal mortality was relatively high in Elizabethan London.

The 154 male as compared to 93 female stillbirths reported from 1609 to 1623 (table 2) at first might seem unlikely. Potter and Adair (1940), however, state that 78 percent of all stillborn fetuses aged less than four months are males, and that although the proportion of females increases as gestation progresses, the overall sex ratio for all stillbirths is 1,303 males to 1,000 females. The ratio for the table 2 totals is 1,243 male to 1,000 females.

There are records of the births of two deformed fetuses, one of them described simply as "A man Child, a verie Deformed Creature" (4 February 1621). A second unfortunate survived only about 16 hours after delivery:

> Sayd chyld beinge deformed was Borne having a face and body in all respects lyke a man chyld saving that the forehed and eyes ded meete togither with a signe of too eyes but it had no eyes and a flate brode nose not beinge hollowe without grisselle therein and under the lefte syde of the nose was a hard lippe as if it weare three beries

joyned togither and it had a nother lipp but it had no jawes in the mouth thereof The body was in good shape and found havinge too armes and too handes and it had fyve fingers and a thomb and each hand it had [was] also too longe but the Right legg from the ankle or shinn bone Downewards ded bend wth the foot inwarde with foote and toes well proportioned this chylde was borne one mondaye in the morning. [5 May 1590]

As already mentioned, a number of the stillborn babies were probably also premature, but this distinction is made in only two entries.

A woman chylde beinge stillbourne and beinge so yonge that it was skant to be deserned [scarcely to be discerned] and beinge the Daughter of Symon Queringe a Toolmaker Dwelling at the signe of the halfe moone in the libertie of eastsmithfield was buried the xxiij^rd daye of may ano 1589.

A marginal note adds, "chyld stilborne beinge but a span [nine inches] long."

A man chyld . . . was buried the ix^th Day of March 1590 being a verie smale thing as it was thought the woman was but a q^tr [quarter] of her tyme gone with the sayd chyld and being Delivered of the sayd chyld in the presente [presence] of M^rs pullett.

This last seems an extraordinarily appropriate name for a sixteenth-century midwife!

There is record of the burial of three midwives:

Susanne Roberts Mydwife, wife to Henry Roberte {sic} beyond ye minories. [10 September 1610]

Emme Smith a Midwife, wife to John Smith in hounsditch. [28 August 1615]

Anne Burnam widow, An Antient Midwife, and a long dweller in our parish. [3 May 1624]

But there is no description of their activities.

The illegitimacy rate appparently was relatively low. In the ten-year period from April 1612 to March 1621 there were 2,663 christenings. Of these babies, 43, or 1.61 percent, are recorded as illegitimate. The clerk suspected illegitimacy in a few other cases but was unsure. As we have seen, he nearly always managed to be remarkably well informed about private matters in the parish. Typical entries for baptism of such babies:

A woman chyld the reputed daughter to Mathew Thorne a curriar this chyld was borne of the boddie of Judith bell a single woman brought a bedd in the howse of Richard Jackson a labourer dwelling in Thomas Pryce his Rentte[5] being in the libertie of Eastsmithfield. [7 February 1598]

Rachel Snelhauke, the reputed daughter of Christopher

5. That is, a house or part of a house rented by Richard Jackson from Thomas Pryce.

Snelhauke Farrier the Mother named Joane Carpenter a single-woman (late servant to Mr John Liddon our deputie deceased) whoe was delivered of the said child under our Church-wall. [26 January 1616]

That is, she was delivered of the child in the open next to the wall of the church—and in the winter! The clerk comments in a similar case, "There are to manie of such Servants now a dayes. more is the pittie" (19 May 1622).

As already mentioned, one of the unusual features of the St. Botolph's records is that for many years the age at death was recorded. Complete figures are available from 1583 to 1599, and we can therefore study survival rates.

Infants dying in the first month after birth were known in Shakespeare's day as *chrisoms*.[6] We can calculate the chrisom death rates for 1584–98 (table 2), again recognizing that 1592 and 1593 were plague years. By contrast, the comparable overall figure for the United States in 1963 was 18.2 deaths per 1,000 live births (Anon. 1965). Thus in sixteenth-century St. Botolph's Parish about nine times as many babies died during the first month as is the case at present in the United States.

Deaths of babies under one year of age including the chrisoms are summarized in table 2 under the heading "Infants." A measure of the devastation of a plague epidemic

6. The term came from the white cloth of the same name that was laid over the baby at baptism (Halliwell 1847).

is reflected in the 1589–93 death rate for infants—349 per 1,000 live births—but the earlier and later rates, 296.0 and 272.3, are also appalling. Comparable rates for 1965, nearly four centuries later, were 23.7 per 1,000 live births for the United States and 19.0 per 1,000 for England and Wales (Anon. 1968).

For various reasons it is not possible to follow each individual in the parish from birth to death, but we can determine how many of the babies christened in a given year survived until, for example, age five. To illustrate: we observe the number of christenings in, say, 1583 and then count how many babies under one year of age died in 1583, how many aged one died in 1584, and so on up to how many aged four died in 1587. Then we examine the total of all these deaths (from 1583 through 1587) in relation to the number christened in 1583 (table 3). This procedure of course ignores possible errors introduced by babies being taken into or out of the parish, but it gives us an approximation. The method also assumes that the numbers of births and deaths were fairly stable from year to year. This obviously was not true when an epidemic occurred.

The fate of the group of babies born during each year can be followed horizontally across the table. Data at the bottom indicate that of every hundred babies born during this period, only about 70 would survive until their first birthday, about 48 to their fifth, and 27–30 to their fifteenth. Of course the population of St. Botolph's parish represents only a

Table 3. Survival to Ages One, Five, Ten, and Fifteen, 1583–99

Year of birth	Total christenings	Total dying before age				Percentage surviving to age			
		1	5	10	15	1	5	10	15
1583	165	38	52	62	95	77.0	68.5	62.5	42.4
1584	161	51	77	131	135	68.3	52.2	18.6	16.1
1585	185	49	79	118	125	73.5	57.3	36.2	32.4
1586	168	42	79	131		75.0	53.0	22.0	
1587	168	65	94	157		61.3	44.0	6.6	
1588	176	47	76	123		73.3	56.8	30.1	
1589	226	70	177	185		69.0	21.7	18.2	
1590	223	55	157	163		75.3	29.6	26.9	
1591	193	49	148			74.6	23.3		
1592	184	56	121			69.6	34.2		
1593	171	118	143			31.0	16.4		
1594	237	66	100			72.2	57.8		
1595	204	42	89			79.4	56.4		
1596	183	67				63.4			
1597	195	55				71.8			
1598	176	41				76.7			
1599	221	52				76.5			
Totals									
1583–99	3,236	963				70.2			
1583–95	2,461		1,292				47.5		
1583–90	1,472			1,070				27.3	
1583–85	511				355				30.5

Note: Italics indicate a plague year, 1593, was involved.

small sample of that of all London, but the mortality figures are shocking. It could be argued that they were made considerably worse by the plague epidemic of 1593, and this is true. However, during the sixty-eight years in which Elizabeth and James reigned, 1558 to 1625, there were plague epidemics in 1563, 1593, 1603, and 1625, an average of once every seventeen years. So one plague epidemic during the period covered by table 3 was all too typical. Plague deaths will be examined further in chapter 5.

Graunt (1759) estimated quite indirectly "that about thirty six per centum of all quick conceptions died before six years old." He had no records of age at death, but based his estimate on those dying

> of the thrush, convulsion, rickets, teeth and worms; and as abortives, chrysomes, infants, livergrown, and overlaid; that is to say, that about ⅓ of the whole [all deaths in the population] died of those diseases, which we guess did all light upon children under four or five years old.

He added half the number of those dying "of the small-pox, swine-pox, and measles, and of worms without convulsions," estimating that of the total number dead from these causes "about ½ might be children under six years old." A recent study (Wrigley 1966) producing life-table mortality rates for the rural village of Colyton, Devon, in the sixteenth and seventeenth centuries showed these rates for infants and children to be much lower than those for St. Botolph's parish.

Finally, Farr has published a life table for Victorian London that enabled Greenwood (1948) to estimate "that about 32% of quick conceptions died before six years old." It is difficult to account for the much higher death rates of infants and children in St. Botolph's Parish. The data seem firm and one can only speculate that factors such as overcrowding, malnutrition, and lack of sanitation were appreciably worse in that parish than in the city as a whole or in rural areas. It should be added that Cowgill (1970) reports that in the city of York in the sixteenth century only about 10 percent of the inhabitants survived to age forty.

I have failed to locate other published studies of mortality rates in sixteenth-century England, although at least one such study is expected soon (Sutherland 1970).

Because age at death was not recorded in the parish after 1599, it is not possible to determine survival rates for older ages. The age distribution at death, excluding deaths ascribed to plague in 1593, appears in table 4. In comparing the number of deaths for each age group it is important to remember that the span of these groups varies from one month (chrissom) to ten years (e.g., age twenty to twenty-nine years).

Other than the very high numbers of infant and child deaths already commented on, the most striking feature of the table is the large numbers of deaths in the twenty to twenty-nine and the thirty to thirty-nine age groups. This phenomenon will be discussed in the chapter on plague.

Table 4. Age at Death, Excluding Plague Deaths, 1583–99

Chrisom	517	20–29	357
2–6 months	308	30–39	386
7–11	114	40–49	282
1 year	312	50–59	239
2	171	60–69	227
3	97	70–79	114
4	64	80–89	97
5–6	106	90–99	29
7–9	71	100 and over	12
10–14	138	Not stated	53
15–19	169		
		Total	3,863

Although we do not know ages at death after 1599, in-dividuals who were buried in 1600–25 were identified as "sonne to," "daughter to," "wife to," "widow," or "single woman," or by occupation. Thus,

Harman wright, sonne to Leanard wright and Agnes his wife. [6 August 1617]

John Jackson a carman. [27 December 1617]

Helen Palmer, wife to one William Palmer. [27 December 1617]

Presumably those persons listed as sons and daughters were too young for employment or marriage, although we lack proof of this. For the period 1600–25 I counted the burials, distributing them in the categories "Son," "Daughter," "Adult Male," "Adult Female" on the basis of the above identifications, although the term *adult* was certainly used rather arbitrarily. Other information about this period does indicate that employment usually came in the early teens, probably by age fourteen or fifteen in many cases. The results of this study appear in table 5.

Thus, in general more sons died than daughters. The exception was 1603, a plague year. In 1600, 1601, 1602, and 1604 combined there were 52.4 percent sons' deaths and 47.6 percent daughters' deaths, but the addition of the 1603 deaths to those for the other four years gives a majority of daughters' deaths for the five-year period. Among the "adults" more females died than males except in 1603; in the years 1600, 1601, 1602 and 1604 combined there were 47.3 percent adult male deaths and 52.7 percent adult female deaths.

The curious sex ratios at death in some plague epidemics will be discussed in chapter 5.

Death from whatever cause did not always come at home. There are notations of the burial of men and women who died in a "cage," a kind of small jail or covered pen.[7] There were several of these cages in or close to the parish.

Henrye Buxton of Aldewarke in Yorkshire who died in the cage next to Aldgate. [19 August 1571]

Thomas Cowley whoe died in the cage. [25 December 1584—Christmas Day]

7. "Two men and a boy were in the cage at Kingston, who had been apprehended overnight under suspicious circumstances" (Charles Dickens, *Oliver Twist*, 1838–39, chap. 31).

Table 5. Burials by Age Group and Sex, 1600–25

Period	Sons	Daughters	Adult males	Adult females	All males	All females	Total, both sexes	Percentage of of Non Adults		Percentage of Adults	
								Sons	Daughters	Adult males	Adult females
1600–04	714	726	722	701	1,436	1,427	2,863	49.6	50.4	50.1	49.9
1605–09	532	497	420	456	952	953	1,905	51.7	48.3	47.9	52.1
1610–14	527	496	376	392	903	888	1,791	51.5	48.5	49.0	51.0
1615–19	513	432	361	398	874	830	1,704	54.3	45.7	47.6	52.4
1620–24	626	546	444	453	1,070	999	2,069	53.4	46.6	49.5	50.5
Total	2,912	2,697	2,323	2,400	5,235	5,097	10,332	51.9	48.1	49.2	50.8
1603 only	445	480	533	490	978	970	1,948	48.1	51.9	52.1	47.9
1625 only	720	641	604	514	1,324	1,155	2,479	52.9	47.1	54.0	46.0

Note: 1603 and 1625 were plague years.

A woman that died in the cage on Tower hill. [5 December 1587]

A younge man that died in the cage on Tower hill. [30 January 1591]

A woman unknowne whoe died in the cage nere white-chapple. [14 December 1595]

William Jones a vagrant whoe died in the cage in East-smithfield. [11 November 1597]

There dyed a woman in the cadge at Tower Hill whose name we knowe not. [17 February 1602]

Death came to others unexpectedly on the street, or in a doorway where they huddled to rest, or in a hayloft where they had crept in sickness. Sometimes only the first name was known. The clerk said what he could as he noted the burial.

Margaritt whoe died by the towne ditche. [2 September 1571]

Grace Butcher whoe dyed on the heighe waye on Tower hill. [14 October 1573]

Robert Badger A butcher whoe died in a little shopp by the Bell [a tavern] on Tower hill. [20 October 1574]

A boye that died in a hayloft att the Red Lyon. [13 August 1581]

A man that died in the streete by the bookshop. [24 September 1581]

Poore Peter found by Eastsmithfield. [16 April 1583]

Robert A vagrant that died in the streete. [19 October 1587]

Elizabeth Hopton who died. in the streete. [4 November 1587]

Christian A vagrant that died at Mrs Crews doore. [11 July 1588]

A striplinge who dyed near the barens of broome[8] upon the hill Right over against [the house of] Jeames Evense a baker being in the liberties of Eastsmithfield whose name as it was not knowne for that we could not learne from whence he ded come he was apareled in a whyt canvas Doblett[9] a Freese Jerkin[10] a payer of Fustian[11] Briches and a payer of blewe colered clothe nether stockes [stockings] and Dyed of the plague and was buried xxix^{th} Day of September ano 1590 being aboute xiiij or xv yeares owld he was no parishioner.

8. Fields of broom.
9. A doublet was a kind of snug jacket, with or without sleeves, extending from the neck to the hips.
10. A variety of jacket or waistcoat. Frieze was a coarse, shaggy, woolen fabric.
11. Cloth of cotton and linen.

Edwarde Ellis a vagrante whoe died in the streete. [8 December 1593]

A younge man not knowne whoe died in a haylofte. [20 January 1594]

A creple that died in the streete before John Awsten's doore. [15 November 1596]

A Poore woman being vagrant whose name was not knowne shee dyed in the striete under the seate before M[r] Christian Shipmans howse called the crowne[12] w[t]hout aldgate an she being in the high striete. And was buried the xxiiij[th] day of Aprill anno 1597. yeares xxiiij she was no parishioner with us neather cowld we learne from whence she came she dyed of the plague.

A mayde a vagrant unknowen whoe died in the streete nere the posternes.[13] [23 July 1597]

Margaritt a deaff woman who died in the streete. [27 September 1597]

A young stripling being vagrant who dyed in Peter Miller's hayloft. [3 November 1597]

A young man in a whyt canvas Dublett & a Rownd payer of Britchis being vagarant and dyed in the streete neare sparrowes corner being in the precinct neare the Tower

12. A tavern.
13. The Postern Gate in the City Wall, close to the Tower.

we colde not learne from whence he did com. [15 November 1597]

A young man vagarant having no abyding place, being in a lether dublet, a black freeze jurkin, and a payer of Russed [russet] gaskens,[14] who dyed in the streete before the dore of Joseph Hayes a braseyer [brazier] dwelling at the signe of Robin hood in the high striete. . . . he was abowte xviij yeares owld I colde not learne his name. [4 February 1597]

Alice Bell a poor child in Swane Alye. [20 August 1603]

John Fare a countreyman lying and dying in ye church-yarde. [4 July 1606]

A poore man who died in a stable whose name wee could not learne. [3 January 1610]

Jane Quyre, an Irish Child who dyed in the street, daughter to an Irish vagrant. [20 November 1611]

Hendrick Sturman a dutchman who dyed in the streete in ye night in his drunkennesse. [22 April 1613]

Many more such reports could be quoted.

Let us now turn to the question of the actual population of London and of St. Botolph's Parish in 1558–1625. Here we immediately discover an almost complete lack of reliable

14. Loose hose.

information. There was no census in those days; the first census was not taken in Great Britain until 1801 (Singer and Underwood 1962). A record of assessments of the inhabitants of London in 1694 does in effect, according to Glass (1966), amount to the first census of that city. Of course very much smaller than it is now, "London, at the accession of James I, was said to contain little more than 150,000 inhabitants" (Angus 1854). Graunt (1759) presents a table showing, he states, "the number of men, women, and children, in the several wards of London, and liberties, taken in August 1631, by special command from the Right Honourable the Lords of his Majesty's Privy Council," but he gives no information about how the data were obtained. The table shows a total population for London of 130,178. Rowse (1951) states that late in the sixteenth century its population "was nearing 300,000 and increasing rapidly."

Regrettably, we also have no firm figures for the number of inhabitants in St. Botolph's Parish—what demographers call "the population at risk"—simply because there is no record of any count of the parish. However, certain indirect information is of value. Graunt (1759) said that in 1631 the Ward of Portsoken had a population of 5,703. Other sources indicate that St. Botolph's Parish included both the Ward of Portsoken and the Liberty of Eastsmithfield (26 April 1622; Williams 1960), but Graunt does not mention this liberty. However, if his data are correct the population of the parish must have exceeded 6,000 in 1631.

Briefly I had hopes that the records of the number of parishioners taking communion on Easter Sunday might give an index to the population. The totals and dates are as follows:

663	20 April 1595
653	27 March 1597
524	16 April 1598
629	8 April 1599
672	23 March 1599[15]

Attendance at Easter communion was compulsory. Church law in 1584 required "attendance at church on Sundays and holy days by everyone, together with the reception of the Holy Communion by all over the age of 16 years" (Brink-worth 1942). Canon 112 of the ecclesiastical law of the Church of England, apparently passed in 1603, stated that

the minister, church-wardens, questmen and assistants of every parish church and chapel shall yearly, within forty days after Easter exhibit to the bishop or his chancellor the names and surnames of all parishioners, as well men as women, which being of the age of sixteen years received not the communion at Easter before. [Phillimore 1895]

Rowse (1951) confirms that these rules were enforced.[16]

15. The new year, 1600, began on 26 March.
16. The St. Botolph records for 1616 and 1617 tell at which public house the bread and wine for each communion were pur-

But the totals of Easter Sunday communicants in 1595–99 are baffling because they clearly represent only a fraction of the parish population aged sixteen or over. The numbers of babies christened in the parish in those years, for example, were 204, 183, 195, 176, and 221, and the corresponding totals for burials were 175, 234, 358, 229, and 259. Such totals certainly must have represented a population base of much more than up to 672 people over the age of sixteen. Graunt (1759) claimed, it will be recalled, that there were 5,703 inhabitants in Portsoken Ward, a part of the parish, in 1631.

Undoubtedly there may have been a few people—secret dissenters, for example—who avoided taking communion and a good many more who were unable to do so because they were under sixteen, or not yet confirmed, or sick, or excommunicated, or even in prison. We know that certain offenders were specifically barred by ecclesiastical law from the communion table. Among these were the "open and notorious evil liver," he who had wronged his neighbor, persons between whom the curate found "malice and hatred to reign," those "openly known to live in sin notorious without repentance," those who refused to kneel during the church

---

chased. When it was the King's Head, operated by a Master I. Scott "neere unto Aldgate," there is a crude sketch of a bird on the margin of the page; for the Chequers, located outside Aldgate and owned by William Wells, vintner, there is the outline of a checker board.

service or otherwise failed to conform to the ritual, and those who "offend their brethren, either by adultery, whoredom, incest or drunkenness, or by swearing, ribaldry, usury, or any other uncleanness, or wickedness of life" (Phillimore 1842). Quite a catalogue of human frailties! No doubt the parish had its share of offenders, some of whom were barred from communion. But we do not know how many.

Canon law also stated, "None shall give the communion to the parishioner of another priest without his manifest licence," exceptions being made for travelers and for persons in danger of death (Phillimore 1842).

London did have a large transient population and in addition received a steady influx of immigrants, chiefly from the country (Gibbons 1969). Graunt (1759) reported:

It is therefore certain that London is supplied with people from out of the country, whereby not only to supply the overplus differences of burials above mentioned, but likewise to increase its inhabitants according to the said increase of housing.

The migration was made possible, Graunt thought, by depletion of the population of towns like Lincoln and Winchester and by an excess in rural areas of christenings over burials. That in London the burials exceeded the christenings in the years 1606–10, 1625, 1630, 1636, etc. (and presumably in the intervening years as well) is shown by data in *Londons Remembrancer* (1665), written by John Bell, Clerk to the

Company of Parish Clerks. This imbalance obtained well into the seventeenth century at least (Angus 1854). Rowse (1951) confirms the migration into London, and there is no reason to doubt that the Parish of St. Botolph without Aldgate also had its immigrants in considerable numbers.

We know that while for the period 1558 to 1625 the number of christenings in the parish was climbing steadily, it was usually exceeded by the number of burials (table 1, fig. 3). This would have resulted in a reduction in the population and a corresponding drop in the death rate had it not been for a considerable immigration into the parish. Actually the annual number of deaths mounted steadily, even in non-plague years, over the whole period. We have information on the numbers of people taking part in the virtually compulsory communions on Easter Sunday, but these numbers seem far less than the parish population aged sixteen and over. We know that transient or immigrant nonmembers of the parish could be christened, married, and sometimes buried there, but they could not receive communion in St. Botolph's. Their number may have been quite large, and certainly they were part of the "population at risk" of the parish. The size of this population remains a mystery; what the "risks" were will be described in the next chapter.

IV: "By What Disease or Casualty"

In London and in England in the latter part of the sixteenth century the treatment of illness and injury was undertaken by a variety of practitioners. Standing highest professionally were the physicians, who cared for sick people but did not operate or otherwise shed blood. Surgery and related procedures, such as bloodletting, were done by surgeons and barber-surgeons, who occupied a lesser although still important rank. Physicians were relatively well educated and trained. Surgeons and barber-surgeons had much less formal education but served long apprenticeships (Garrison 1929; Poynter 1948). Finally, there was a great number of untrained practitioners and quacks who couched cataracts, cut for stone and hernia, pulled teeth, opened boils, applied poultices, administered purges, and so on, too often leaving a wake of misery and mistreatment.

Legislation under Henry VIII required that

> no person within the city of London, nor within seven miles of the same, shall take upon him to exercise and occupy as a physician or surgeon, except he be first examined, approved, and admitted by the bishop of London, or by the dean of St. Paul's for the time being, calling to him or them four doctors of physic, and for surgery other expert persons in that faculty.

Persons treating patients without having passed the examination would pay a fine of five pounds for every month that they were in violation (3 Hen. 8, cap. 11; Phillimore 1842). Eleven years later, in 1522, the physicians in London and within seven miles of the city were incorporated by royal edict and given the power to examine candidates for practice themselves; surgeons had to be examined by the bishop or his vicar-general (14 & 15 Hen. 8, cap. 5). In 1540 London's barbers and surgeons were incorporated as one body (32 Hen. 8, cap. 42), the United Barber-Surgeon Company (Garrison 1929).

There was a severe shortage of physicians and surgeons, and to make matters worse, a good many of these men apparently were interested only in patients who could pay high fees (Copeman 1960; Smith 1940). Therefore the act of 1511 which had been passed in the effort to improve professional standards and "for the avoiding of sorceries, witchcraft, and other inconveniences" was modified in 1542–43 by a new law (34 & 35 Hen. 8, cap. 8). The latter recognized that since the previous legislation had been enacted,

> the company and fellowship of surgeons in London, minding only their own lucres, and nothing the profit or ease of the diseased or patient, have sued and troubled divers honest persons, as well men as women, whom God hath endued with the knowledge of the nature, kind and operation of certain herbs, roots, and waters, and the using and ministering of them to such as be pained with customable [habitual, chronic] diseases, as women's breasts being sore, a pin and the web in the eye,[1] uncomes[2] of hands, burning, scaldings, sore mouths, the stone,[3] strangury,[4] saucelim,[5] morphew,[6] and such other like diseases.

In other words, the surgeons were accused of reducing professional competition by prosecuting honest laymen who, although untrained, could treat many diseases. The competence of the surgeons was questioned:

> For although the most part of the persons of the said craft of surgeons have small cunning, yet they will take great

1. A growth of the conjunctiva obscuring vision.
2. Ulcers, whitlows.
3. Calculus in the bladder.
4. Difficult urination.
5. Facial eruption.
6. Disease of the skin of the face.

sums of money and do little therefore, and by reason thereof they do oftentimes impair and hurt their patients rather than do them good.

Therefore "every person being the king's subject, having knowledge and experience of the nature of herbs, roots and waters, or of the operation of the same" was authorized to treat a variety of diseases and conditions "without suit, trouble, penalty, or loss of their goods" (Phillimore 1842).

The criticisms directed at the surgeons no doubt were well founded, and the need for inexpensive care of the indigent poor was great (Copeman 1960; Gibbons 1969), but matters were not to be improved very much by, in effect, permitting laymen to practice medicine. Some of these people, particularly in rural areas, probably were skilled and conscientious (Roberts 1962). Many others were not only ignorant but callous and rapacious. William Clowes (1544–1604), Surgeon to the Fleet and also to the Queen, a leading member of his profession and obviously prejudiced, in 1585 poured out the vials of his wrath upon "this beastly broode," the quacks,

which doe forsake their honest trades, whereunto God hath called them, & do daily rush into Phisicke & Chirurgerie. And some of them be Painters, some Glasiers, some Tailors, some Wevers, some Joiners, some Cutlers, some Cookes, some Bakers & some Chandlers &c. Yea, now a daies it is to appara[n]t to see how Tinkers, Tooth-drawers, Pedlers, Ostlers, Carters, Porters, Horse-gelders, horse-leeches, Ideots, Apple-squires [pimps], Broomemen, bawds, witches, cuniuerers [conjurers], South-saiers, & sow gelders, Roages, Rat-catchers, Ru[n]agates, & Procters of Spitlehouses [houses for the sick], with such other lyke rotten & stincking weeds, which do in town & countrie, without order, honestie, or skil, daily abuse both Phisick & Chirurgerie, having no more perseverance, reason, or knowledge in this art, the[n] hath a goose.

The story of attempts to regulate medical practice in England in the sixteenth and seventeenth centuries is told in detail by Roberts (1962, 1964).

St. Botolph's parish had a few doctors. The record books note the burials of several.

Mr Daniel Muller physition, a Stranger borne. [31 May 1617]

Mr John Keitley a Physition, who lodged in the House of Mrs Annabell Cockes Widow of Hounsditch. [16 September 1623]

Nathaniel Thorey Grocer free[man] of the Barbour-Chiurgions.[7] [19 July 1623]

Richard Foster Citizen and Barbour-Chiurgion. [5 September 1624]

7. That is, a member of the Barber-Surgeons' Company. He may not himself have been a barber-surgeon; it was possible by this time to belong to a guild for social reasons without practicing its trade or specialty.

Owen Fle———ch [spelling uncertain] barber surgeon. [15 July 1625]

One individual who practiced surgery illegally got into trouble.

Memerandum that M^r xpopher [Christopher] Threlkeld our minister ded denounce in our parish church on Sunday being the xxijnd Day of June ano 1595 one Thomas Woodhouse to be excomunicated from the church and congregation by vertue of an Inhibition for the same from Mr Edward Stanhop channcelor to the bishrip of London dated the xiiijth Day of June Ano 1595.

The clerk's marginal notation adds, "this was for using of chiurgerie and not being admitted so to do." It will be recalled that it was the bishop who licensed surgeons to treat patients.

There are not many accounts of actual surgical practice, but we know of one because the clerk was involved, and for a curious reason. Note that he does not hide his contempt for the surgeons.

Memorandum that M^{rs} [blank space] Tyre alijs Calias, formerly Ruttum who hath had of a longe tyme a sore hand by a Fellon[8] upon which cure dyvers surgions, and others who have proved there conninge to hir great payne and grieffe, but no holpe [help] could be had. In consid-

8. An infection or abscess at the tip of the finger.

eration whereof the said hand being hir Ryght hand, was by the advyce of surgions cut or sawed offe on wedensday in the morning being the xj day of August ano 1596 and the said hand was by me Thomas harrydance being the parish clarke in the presents of Thomas ponder being the sexten Buried Right before the dore within the Sowth churchyeard the said Wednesday being the xjth day of August Anno 1596 abowte the ower of eyght of the clocke in the morning Thus god send hir good Rest and ease or healp after the same if it be gods good will and pleasure.

Surgeons sometimes branched out into medical practice (Copeman 1960; Roberts 1964). We see an example of this in the case of a young man treated for syphilis. The clerk, incidentally, does not use this term, but refers first to "some desease" and then to *de Morbo gallico,* "from the French disease," as the cause of death. He records the burial of

Jhon Akenhead a tapster late dwelling at the signe of the greyhownd in southwarke[9] who for some desease was to be cured by one M^r foster A chiurgion and did lye at [was lodged at] the house of Ellen wryght a widow dwelling in a garden howse neare hogg lane in the precinct near whyt chaple barres[10] where he dyed and was Buried the second day of februarie Anno 1599 yeares xxv. he was no parishioner with us.————de Morbo gallico.

9. A district across the Thames from the Parish of St. Botolph without Aldgate.
10. See figs. 1 and 2.

As usual, the clerk knew the details.

On 26 January 1617 the parish buried

> Anne Wittles, als [alias] Philips, sometime wife to Augustine Philips one of the Kinges players, shee departed this life in the house of William Smith Surgion of Hounsditch.

We can assume she was being treated at the surgeon's house.

There is also record of the burial on 5 May 1621 of "Christopher Hayward, a Pettifogger, of Squirrell alley, and a verie Thrid-bare felloe . . . he died by Bleeding." This probably referred to the common procedure of phlebotomy, the letting of blood for supposedly therapeutic reasons. It could be overdone.

"Physic" of course meant medicine, but the several "Professors of Physic"—one of them a woman—who went to their rewards while resident in the parish were clearly quacks using a title that made them sound like physicians.

> Mr David warde, a professor of phisicke of East Smithfield. [30 March 1616]

> Margret Mott, (a Counterfeit Physition, and Surgion) wife to William Mott, Silkweaver of hatchett alley . . . an old Quacksalver.[11] [2 February 1617]

> Elizabeth Martin wife to John Martin a professor of Physick and Chiurgerie. [23 July 1623]

11. This word probably comes from two Dutch words meaning *quack* and *salve,* that is, one who boasts noisily about his ointments. Our term *quack* is a contraction (Craigie 1914).

Edward Askew a poore-man, professor of Phisick, who lodged in the house of John Clarke a Taylor in Rosemarie Lane. [15 June 1624]

Mr Mathias Evans A Professor of Phisick and other Curious Arts who dwelt in the Minories street. [5 July 1625]

A special collection was taken in the parish church on 5 June 1587

towarde the curring of one Robert Raye who was a younge man Borne in this parishe and is now Dwelling in Whight Chapell . . . Beinge trobled with the faling sicknes the some of fower shillings.

This was a rather large sum, and of course the cure of "faling sicknes," or epilepsy, was not within the skill of either physician or quack. There is no further information.

Very little is said in the clerk's books about sanitation, although reference has been made to the offices of scavenger and raker. One episode is in the record because a special vestry meeting was held on Monday, 10 October 1599. It seems that several tenants living on property owned by the church had made a "Suplycation . . . to the L. [Lord] Maior & the benche to have a comon privie contrarie to there Leases." In other words, the leases did not promise a privy. If it were provided, the vestrymen would have to find the money. Master Alderman Hallyday of the Ward of Portsoken took the matter up with the vestry. The counterpanes of the leases[12] were examined by the vestrymen, and

> it was thought good that answer shold be made to the alderman that if the tenants did suppose that the parish weare by there Leases Inioyned to make them a comon privie that they shold comence there action agaynst the parishe and the parishe wold answer by Law et c.

The next day the parish clerk delivered the counterpanes to Master Nicholas Reynolds, the alderman's deputy. On 18 October eight parish freeholders, or property owners, including several churchwardens inspected fourteen properties occupied by the dissatisfied tenants. The vestry decided to build privies for four of the properties and to repair the "house of office" of a fifth. This would seem a niggardly settlement by modern standards, but at least it was an improvement.

The problem of disease entities in Elizabethan England is as fascinating as it is complex. The number of recognized, fairly definite diseases of course was relatively small. Diagnoses, even when made by experienced physicians, were not necessarily correct. Looking back from our own more en-

12. An indenture is a mutual agreement made by two parties. In earlier days identical copies were written on the same sheet of parchment and were then separated by cutting an irregular line between them. Or the copies were written on separate sheets and then they were held together and a jagged line was cut on both. (To *indent* comes from the Latin words *in* and *dens,* a tooth.) In either case, one edge of each copy matched the other. The duplicate copy was the *counterpane,* in this case held by the parish.

lightened if still imperfect times, we recognize that a fundamental problem was the relatively primitive understanding
of sickness in Shakespeare's day (Copeman 1960). Illness
could, for example, be traced to the influence of the planets
or to an imbalance of the humors—black bile, yellow bile,
blood, and phlegm. Sometimes death was ascribed to what
we would recognize as a symptom rather than a disease;
people were said, for example, to die of dropsy.

If by our standards the medical man's idea of disease was
not necessarily clear or correct, the layman of course was even
more in the dark. The information in the St. Botolph records
on the "cause" of death of those who were buried there was
obtained by laymen from laymen and was written down by
other laymen. Graunt (1759) explains:

> When anyone dies, then, either by tolling,[13] or ringing
> of a bell, or by bespeaking of a grave of the sexton, the
> same is known to the searchers, corresponding with the
> said sexton. The searchers hereupon (who are antient
> matrons, sworn to their office) repair to the place where the
> dead corps lies, and by view of the same, and by other
> enquiries, they examine by what disease or casualty the
> corps died. Hereupon they make their report to the parish
> clerk.

The St. Botolph record book tells of a single scandalous
instance when the searchers were *not* called.

13. Hence John Donne's (1572–1631) admonition, "And therefore never send to knowe for whome the bell tolls; It tolls for thee."

Memorandum that Elizabeth Prettie a mayden did lye at the house of Thomas Huland a saylor dwelling in Morlyes rentte being in the libertie of Eastsmithfield where she dyed, and contrarie to the good and decent order apoynted by the Queenes ma^{tie} the search was not made by our searchers apoynted and sworne for the said purpose nor yet was thee before knowledge given to the minister or clarke of this parish. Carried thorowghe the posterne of the cittie and so up . . . unto the parish church of St Peters the poore being in broad street and there without any search after a sermon made by one Mr Pratt a minister she was Buried in the church yeard of the said parishe of St Peters the poore the vth Day of August Anno 1596. yeares [age] xx.

It is further noted, "But whereof she dyed I do not knowe." The Parish of St. Botolph without Aldgate had to pay the funeral charges, 2s. 9d., because she died there. This must have rankled, particularly in what the clerk implies was a very suspicious case. He seems to have sought details with his usual thoroughness but not to have been prepared to make an accusation.

John Graunt did not have much confidence in the reliability of

the old-women searchers [who] after the mist of a cup of ale, and the bribe of a two-groat[14] fee, instead of one, given them, cannot tell whether this emaciation or lean-

14. A groat was a silver coin worth fourpence.

ness were from a phthisis[15] or from an hectic fever, atrophy, &c.

John Bell, Clerk to the Company of Parish Clerks of London, defended the searchers a few years later in his *Londons Remembrancer* (1665).

> True and undeniable it is, That the *Searchers* are generally ancient women, and I think are therefore most fit for that office: But sure I am they are chosen by some of the eminentest men of the Parish to which they stand related; and if any of their choosers should speak against their abilities, they would much disparage their own Judgments. And after such Choice they are examined touching their sufficiency, and sworn to that Office by the Dean of the Arches,[16] or some Justices of the Peace, as the cause shall require.

Almost a hundred years later Thomas Birch (1759), discussing the bills of mortality, commented sensibly:

> The low capacity of the person usually chosen into this office [searcher] has been made an objection to the truth and justness of the bills. But with regard to natural deaths, there seems no other capacity in these searchers than that of relating what they hear. For the wisest person in the

15. Wasting disease.
16. The judge of the Court of Arches, which had jurisdiction over certain London parishes under the Archbishop of Canterbury.

parish would be able to find out very few distempers from a bare inspection of the dead body, and could only bring back such an account, as the family and friends of the deceased would be pleased to give.

The searchers no doubt did on occasion accept a bribe, probably most often to conceal a case of plague because of the quarantine and other restrictions that would be imposed on others in the house if this disease were reported. The searchers' job was unpleasant at best and perilous often enough,[17] and perhaps the "mist of a cup of ale" seemed to help. Birch, however, has put his finger on the real difficulty. Even if the body were examined by an experienced physician instead of an ignorant old woman, the physician would be largely dependent on what he could learn from family and neighbors. There is no mention of autopsies. Furthermore, of course, the diagnosis would still be in terms of sixteenth-century concepts of disease.

Table 6 summarizes the "causes" of 4,253 deaths as set down by the clerk in recording all burials in the Parish of St. Botolph without Aldgate from 1583 through 1599. For an additional 700 burials put on the record during those years and in that parish, no "cause" was specified. Reliability of the alleged reason for death ranges all the way from excellent for, say, the executions, to good for "plague" (but undoubtedly additional plague cases were ascribed to other causes), to very dubious indeed for such a condition as "fever,"* which is not a

17. Brett-James 1935; Kargon 1963; Wilson 1927.

disease. Rather than list each "cause" by its variant spellings, I have modernized the latter. Plague, and deaths by accident and violence, will be separately considered in later chapters.

Table 6. "Causes" of 4,253 Deaths in Order of Frequency, 1583–99

"Cause"[a]	No. of Deaths	Percent
Plague	1,167	23.6
Con[b]	1,101	22.2
Not stated	700	14.1
Pining, long sick	656	13.2
Ague	300	6.1
Flux, scouring	126	2.5
Smallpox, pox	117	2.4
Childbed	76	1.5
Teeth	53	1.1
Impostume	51	1.0
Surfeit	49	1.0
		88.7%
Great age	43	
Worms	42	
Dropsy	40	
Accidents	31	
Bleach	31	
Purples	30	
Sore leg or arm	26	
Planet	22	
Thought	21	
Yellow jaundice	21	
Bruise	17	
Murder, violence	17	
Measles	16	
Rupture	16	

a. Stillbirths are not included.
b. Abbreviation for consumption or convulsions—or perhaps for both.

"Cause"	No. of Deaths
Scurvy	16
Colic	14
Fever	12
French pox	12
Died suddenly	10
Jaw-fallen	10
Pleurisy	8
Palsy	8
Swine pox	7
Executed	6
Sore mouth, canker	6
Black jaundice	5
King's evil, Queen's evil	5
Sore feet, toes off	5
Stone, gravel	5
Falling sickness	4
Fistula	4
Tympany, wind colic	4
Gout	3
Mother	3
Mumps	3
[Postoperative]	3
Scald head	3
Spleen	3
Strangullion	3
Suicide	3
Chin cough	2
Wolf	2
Boils	1
Canker of privities	1
Cough	1
Found dead	1
Frenzy	1
Green sickness	1
Heaving of lights	1
Issue of blood	1

"Cause"	No. of Deaths
Murr, catarrh	1
Old wound	1
Piles	1
Sore hand	1
Starvation	1
Water issue	1

Table 7 shows the distribution by age groups of a number of the more common "causes." If no age was recorded by the parish clerk, the individual was assigned to the "Child" or "Adult" category on the basis of the context of the burial record. Table 8 indicates the distribution by calendar year of selected "causes."

"Con," listed as the reason for 1,101 deaths, is a frustrating abbreviation because we cannot be sure whether it stands for "consumption," or "convulsions," or both. Early lists based on the bills of mortality[18] all show consumption to be a much more common cause of death than convulsions. This is one argument for thinking that "con" referred to the lung disease. Another reason is that "con" had a fairly even distribution through all age groups (see table 7) rather than occurring mostly in young children, as Birch (1759) reported was true of "convulsions."

"Pining" and "long sick" need no explanation; the terms obviously describe the patient's course rather than his disease.

18. Anon. 1665; Birch 1759; Graunt 1759.

Table 7. Selected "Causes" of Death by Age Group, 1583–99

Age Group	Con[a]	Ague	Flux, scouring	Smallpox, pox	Childbed	Teeth	Imposthume	Surfeit	Worms	Dropsy	Bleach	Purples	Planet	Thought
Chrisom	20					9								
2–6 months	71	5		8		7	1		4		15	1	2	
7–11	16	4	8	9		29	1		3		2		2	
1 year	81	15	6	24		5	3		7		1	1	3	
2	39	10	6	14		1	2		6		1	2	2	
3	18	10	2	14		1			5		3	2	3	
4	17	3		6		1		1	2		1	1	1	
5–6	20	13	4	8			1		6			2	2	
7–9	17	9	4	7			1		3		2	1	2	
10–14	42	15	6	7			1	2	3	4		1		
15–19	50	26	15	8	1		4	2	1	6		3	3	
20–29	94	59	10	7	27		8	13	2	8	3	3	1	4
30–39	127	42	19	2	39		8	9		10		3		4
40–49	116	41	19	2	8		8	9		8	1	4	1	5
50–59	101	32	7	1			3	5		2		3		5
60–69	112	13	15				8	5			1	2		2
70–79	67	2	1				2	1						1
80–89	53		1							1				
90–99	18											1		
100 and over	7										1			
Child	2	1								1				
Adult	13		3		1			2						
Totals	1,101	300	126	117	76	53	51	49	42	40	31	30	22	21

a. See Table 6.

Table 8. Selected "Causes" of Death by Year, 1583–99

Year	Con.[a]	Ague	Flux, scouring	Smallpox, pox	Childbed	Teeth	Imposthume	Surfeit	Worms	Dropsy	Bleach	Purples	Planet	T'bought
1583	101		1	1	2		2	2		1		1		
1584	85		1	5	9		1	2	3					1
1585	84		2	1	4		4			1				
1586	123			5	2		2	1	1	1		2		
1587	151	39	3	4	2			1				3		
1588	69	30	3	2	3			2						
1589	80	24	2	1	2		4	3		2	1			
1590	46	12		5	3		4	2						
1591	61	11	1	2	4	2	3	2	1					
1592	50	65	5	5	7	17	6	2	5	3	2	1	1	1
1593	46	34	2	5	5	4	6	11	12	9	7	2	16	3
1594	31	5	1	21	5	1	1	9	4	6	4		3	3
1595	30	21	2	6	8	5	3	5	2		6			2
1596	27	18	3	13	3		4	3	3	5	6			3
1597	44	37	33	4	9	12		3	1	7	4	17	1	5
1598	37	3	42	4	3	12	8	2	3	1	1	2	1	2
1599	36	1	26	36	5		3	2	7	4		2		1
Totals	1,101	300	126	117	76	53	51	49	42	40	31	30	22	21

a. See Table 6.

"Ague" or "burning ague" apparently referred to an acute, perhaps intermittent, fever with chills and shaking (Murray 1818).

"Flux," "scouring," or "bloody flux" in most cases probably indicated dysentery. The appalling contamination of water and food would be expected to make this a common type of disease, particularly in the warm months (Copeman 1960). The numerous cases in 1597–99 may represent an epidemic. Other types of discharge were sometimes indicated. There is an entry on 25 August 1595 for the burial of a nineteen-year-old girl who "dyed with over Mutch bleeding at the nose in her sicknes." A marginal notation adds, "of a flux of blood." This possibly was a case of vicarious menstruation.

"Smallpox" and "pox" have been combined in one category because it appears that the parish clerks probably used them synonymously. Pox was sometimes an Elizabethan term for syphilis, also called the great pox to distinguish it from the smallpox. There are several reasons for thinking that the clerks of St. Botolph's meant smallpox when they spoke of "the pockes." One is that 90 of the 117 cases in which the disease is supposed to have resulted in death occurred in children under ten years of age (table 7). Survivors quite probably acquired immunity. Another is that in 1583, 1584, 1585, and part of 1586 the clerks mentioned eight deaths supposedly due to pox without referring at all to smallpox. After that date the latter term was always used except in three instances. "French pox" or, more commonly, *morbus*

Gallicus, the clerks' names for syphilis, were given as a cause of death once in 1585, twice in 1587, and nine times in 1594–99. Syphilis was the only disease named in Latin by the clerk, perhaps as a euphemism, e.g., in the record of the burial of a twenty-year-old girl, "con[sumpta] cu[m] morbo gallico," consumed by the French disease (1 June 1599). Graunt (1759) believed that many deaths from this "too frequent malady" were not reported as such. The same may have been true of smallpox, which certainly was prevalent in the days of Elizabeth (Copeman 1960).

Swine pox (eight deaths) is said to have been in Tudor times a name for what we call chicken pox (Neilson 1948).

There are reports of 76 deaths in childbed in 1583–99. During the same period there were 3,236 christenings. This is equivalent to a maternal death rate of 23.5 per 1,000 deliveries. Such a rate is of course high by the most modern standards, although not by those of a few decades ago. In 1968 the maternal mortality rate in England and Wales was 0.2 per thousand (Barron 1968). The parish records give no clue as to the cause of the deaths in childbirth except for three or four cases when it was noted that the woman also had plague, or stone, or colic. Midwifery in Shakespeare's day, with a few notable exceptions, was still at a very low level (Forbes 1966), and childbirth was hazardous. At least one of the deaths listed as occurring in childbirth was actually postpartum—"a greene [recently delivered] woman latlye browght a bedd & therefore accownted as in chyldbed" (15 April 1594).

"Teeth" or "breeding of yᵉ teeth" was held responsible for the deaths of 53 babies and small children. This "cause" was not mentioned at all until 1592. "Breeding" in this case meant producing or generating (Murray 1888), possibly reflecting an erroneous notion that teeth are formed shortly before they erupt.

> About the seventh month, sometime more sometime lesse, after the byrth, it is natural for a childe for to breede teeth, in whiche time many one is sore vexed with sondry diseases and paines.

So Thomas Phayer (1510?–60) in *The Booke of Children* (1553). He does not state that there is ever a fatal outcome. When "teeth" was given by the searchers as the cause of death, once again the error was seizing on a conspicuous symptom. The deciduous or milk teeth normally erupt between the ages of six months and two and a half years. Fifty of the 53 deaths were of children under three; the others were of children who were a little older (table 7).

Various kinds of abscesses were known as "impostumes," a term now obsolete—"dyed of an Impostome which Issued out at his eare" (27 July 1592). Impostumes seem to have occurred more commonly in adults. This was also true for "surfeit," a condition supposedly brought on by excessive eating or drinking.

> Peter Yeop being a stearman [steersman?] borne in Skee Dam in Holland whose dwellinge was in Altener neare

> Hamboroughe and beinge Dronke at the house of George Jhonson a carter Dwellinge in the libertie of Eastsmithfield where he endid his lyfe of a surfett with Drenke and was Buried the xxiij[th] Day of Febrewarie ano 1588. beinge no parishioner yeares xxxiiij.

Here again we note the clerk's thoroughness in obtaining the necessary information, even about a foreign sailor.

"Great age" was reported as the cause of death of 43 persons. Twelve of these allegedly lived from 100 up to 110 years!

> Joane Blackborne a poore widow, reported to be above an hundred yeares old. [2 November 1622]

There is no further documentation. It is reassuring to have some indication that a small number of hardy souls survived just about everything the sixteenth century could offer—no mean achievement. The prize for longevity, if the record is to be believed, must go to "Agnis Sadler widdow of the age of 126 yeares." She was buried 26 April 1575.

A not infrequent "cause" of death in babies and children was "y[e] wormes," probably a rather common affliction (Copeman 1960) because of the general lack of sanitation. This term in past centuries could also refer to a tumor or abscess supposedly engendered by, and shaped like, a worm (Murray 1888).

Dropsy (listed only for adults) is, as previously mentioned, a symptom rather than a disease. It was seldom reported until

1592. The frequency with which it was specified after that date possibly reflects the searchers' efforts to be more descriptive. "Tympany" (table 6) described the drumlike condition that develops when an excessive amount of gas or air accumulates in the abdomen. Tympany was regarded as a form of dropsy (Quincy 1722).

"Bleach" and "scald" or "scald head" were two ill-defined skin diseases.[19] "Bleach" caused a whitening of the skin, and hence sometimes inspired a false diagnosis of leprosy. (I did not encounter the latter term in the St. Botolph records.) "Scald" is probably a variant of "scalled" or scaled, scaly. Phayer (1553) comments,

> The heads of children are oftentimes ulcered and scalled, as well when they sucke, and then most commonly by reason of sharpe milke, as also when they have bene wayned, and can goe alone.

Other causes included

> an evil complexion of humours by eating of rawe fruite, or other evill meats, and sometime by long continuing in the sunne.

Scald head was characterized by scurf or scabbiness and may sometimes have constituted what we now call ringworm (Barnet 1968). A third skin affliction, "byles" (boils), was listed in one death.

"Measles" was not uncommon in babies and children

19. Halliwell 1847; Murray 1888; Neilson 1948.

(Copeman 1960). Phayer (1553) lumped together "small Pockes and Measels. This disease is comon and familier." Measles to the Elizabethans was not the specific disease we know, but simply a condition in which the skin had spots or pustules. Whooping cough was also known as "chincowgh" (Copeman 1960; Murray 1888). Tetanus or lockjaw went by the curious name "jawfallen." "King's evil" or "Queen's evil," so called because the touch of the monarch was supposed to be a cure, was scrofula, or tuberculosis of the lymph nodes of the neck. Culpeper (1652) spoke of "the imposthumes of the throat, commonly called the King's evil." "Wolf" apparently meant some form of what we call lupus (Latin for wolf); "he dyed of a dezease caled a wolfe" (16 November 1595). "Green sickness" referred to what would now be regarded as a form of anemia in girls.

"Purples" was probably one or more of the varieties of what we now call purpura (Latin for purple). Purplish or livid spots in the skin are typical. The term could also refer to the characteristic lesion of the plague (Murray 1888), and might have been used as a euphemism to conceal plague cases. But this seems unlikely, since purples is cited only thirty times. "Bruise" may have referred to purpuralike lesions.

In May, June, and July of 1589 no less than nineteen babies under the age of three died "pining." No cause is given for what appears to have been a minor epidemic.

Respiratory diseases in addition to consumption occurred.

A four-year-old girl died "of the cough of the lounges [lungs]" (18 April 1597). A man of sixty died "of a cold murr [catarrh]" (30 November 1584), and a man of forty died rather mysteriously "of a strayne or Breuse wch grewe to a pluresye" (22 April 1588).

Reference was made earlier to "strangurie" or "strangullion," urinary retention; it is cited only three times. The "stone" or "gravel," a very common disease of the period (Copeman 1960), is also listed as a cause of death. It usually afflicted adults, but was reported as resulting in the death of a nine-year-old boy (16 February 1596).

Individuals sometimes died suddenly, as they do today. Death could come on the street or at home. A not unusual explanation was that the victim had been "taken in a planet" or "taken under a planet." Of 22 such instances, all but four occurred in 1593. This was a plague year. Deaths "under a planet," like those from plague, were distributed through the year and were most numerous in July and August, but no further parallel is evident. Seventeen of the planet fatalities were children under ten years of age, and seventeen of the deaths (not necessarily the same seventeen) occurred in males. "Taken in a planet" is probably related to the terms "planet struck" and "moon struck," that is, the victim was thought to be suddenly smitten by the hostile influence of a planet. This of course is pure astrology.

The term was sometimes applied in rapid paralytic seizures (Murray 1888; J. Wright 1903; T. Wright 1857). (The word *stroke* popularly refers even now to a sudden attack of illness, as in sunstroke or stroke of apoplexy.) The St. Botolph record tells of the burial of a five-year-old girl "taken lame wth a plannet" (9 February 1593). In *Hamlet,* probably written in 1598–1601, Marcellus (act I, scene 1) speaks of the season

> Wherein our Saviour's birth is celebrated,
> The bird of dawning singeth all night long:
> And then, they say, no spirit dare stir abroad:
> The nights are wholesome; then no planets strike.

A seventeenth-century physician, Nicholas Culpeper (1657), sheds light on this illness when he writes of what he terms catalepsy,

> called in Latine *Occupatio,* detention, and *Deprehensio;* Moderne Writers call it *Congelatio;* in English it is called congelation, or taking, and by the ignorant struck with a Planet.
>
> It is a sudden detention and taking both of body and mind, both sense and moving being lost, the sick remaining in the same figure of body wherein he was taken; whether he sit or lie, or whether his mouth and eyes were open or shut, as they are taken in the disease so they remaine.

Occupatio means violent seizure; *deprehensio,* to be caught unaware; *congelatio,* freezing.

Graunt (1759) touches on the concept when he discusses the fundamental issue of whether the searchers reported the most prominent symptom or the actual cause of death.

I say, it is enough, if we know from the searchers but the most predominant symptoms; as that one died of the head-ach, who was sorely tormented with it, though the physicians were of opinion, that the disease was in the stomach. Again, if one died suddenly, the matter is not great, whether it be reported in the bills [of mortality], suddenly, apoplexy, or planet-strucken, &c.

The sore legs, feet, toes, hands, mouths, and so on to which death was often ascribed must have been due to a wide variety of diseases. Infections were probably common.

Long sick and having sore fiete. [23 July 1597]
He dyed of an Infirmetie in both his feete—sore feete. [6 May 1598]
Sorr Legg. [5 June 1596]
She dyed of a canker in her mouth—sore mouth. [20 October 1592]
Of an owld sore being hurte in service having beene a sowldier. [17 March 1596]

Hemorrhoids and fistulas are mentioned. Inguinal hernias (Cock 1926; Murray 1888) were not uncommon—"beinge bursten [ruptured]" (15 January 1586); "being a bursten man of a rupture in his codde [scrotum]" (21 August 1591).

Two reasons were given for the death of a thirty-six-year-old man: "of a rupture or a wenn [a sebaceous cyst] in his neck" (9 October 1593).

Surgery of the day being what it was, it is surprising that so few postoperative deaths are reported as such. Perhaps the reason was that the poor people who made up most of the Parish of St. Botolph without Aldgate were seldom attended by surgeons. Some fatalities followed operations to remove stones from the bladder. "Stone" or "gravel" was a common and painful disease.

> Memerandum that S^r [Sir] William Winter Knyght Endid this Lyfe in his howse in this parishe the 20th daye of februarie Ano 1588 att eleven of the clocke in the nyght beinge Cutt of the collick and the stone.

The next day, 21 February, it was recorded that

> the Bowells of Sr William Wenter knyght weare by Thomas Ponder ower sexton Buried on the north syde of the churche in the churchyard the xxith Daye of Februarie ano 1588.

Sir William Wynter, or Winter, was a well-known admiral (Laughton 1909).

> Being cutt of ye collick & stone. [27 October 1590]
> He dyed being newe cut of ye stone. [22 April 1592]

Other reasons for surgery were given.

Henry gravens howsholder & coop[er] who dyed of a
sore legg wch legg was by certain surgeannts [surgeons]
cut of on a shroft [Shrove] tewsdaye not one howre before
he departed this Liff. [8 February 1580]

Of a wenn being cutt by surgions. [28 April 1584]

Of a sore hand by the prick w^t a pinn wch lately was sawed
of by surgeions 30 August. [1596]

Sometimes we are only told that the victim "lay at surgery" when he died. In at least one case (26 March 1600) it
was a barber-surgeon who had operated.

Elizabeth came to her throne on 17 November 1558. The
date was celebrated annually thereafter. One way of making
the day momentous was to fire the cannon at the Tower,
probably as a procession passed on the Thames. Gunpowder
was not yet familiar. In 1597 there was an accident and a
bystander was hurt.

Jhon Bowes a weaver he did dwell at Stepnie[20] & being
hurte in the legg with a peece of a chamber[21] which was
shott off at the tryoumphe made at the Tower hill on the
xvij^th day of November Last and having had his legg taken
off by surgions did lye at surgerie at the howse of Edward
Shakelock a minstrell dwelling in the whyt beare alley

20. A district near the Tower.
21. A small cannon for firing salutes which had no carriage but
rested on its breech. In this case the chamber burst.

being in the high striete where he dyed and was Buried the xxv[th] day of November Anno 1597 yeares xxx.

The London hospitals at the time were totally inadequate, and sick people had to be lodged in private homes. This was why the unfortunate John Bowes "did lye at surgerie" in a minstrel's house. Other accidents with guns and gunpowder will be discussed in a later chapter.

Neurological diseases listed as "causes" of death included palsy and falling sickness or epilepsy.

Strange ideas about the uterus, or "mother," as it was sometimes called, persisted into the seventeenth century and beyond. Disturbances of the mother were thought to give rise to hysteria,[22] and sometimes this condition was also called mother.[23] Hysteria was believed to be associated with a swelling or rising of the uterus and, sometimes, with resulting sensations of respiratory difficulty and suffocation. This is reflected in an account of the burial on 6 April 1594 of a nineteen-year-old girl whose death was ascribed to "the heaving of the lounge [lung] called the mother." "Lights" was another name for lungs; "heaving of lights" was also a presumed cause of death. A woman of seventy "dyed sodanly of y[e] mother or yelowe jaunders" (22 December 1590).

22. The term *hysteria* is derived from the Greek word for uterus. It was only later that someone pointed out that men can also become hysterical.

23. Murray 1888; Neilson 1948; Rosen 1968; Wright 1857.

"Spleen" was the alleged cause of three deaths. It referred to severe depression and reflected once again the humoral theory of disease. Spleen is cited in the record books without explanation.

Serious depression, anxiety, or concern was described more commonly as "thowght" or "taken in a thowght."[24] It is stated or implied as the cause of death of eleven men and ten women. The youngest were twenty years old (table 7). The best known was Christopher Threlkeld, a curate of the parish (see chap. 2). The first account is of a countryman who met tragedy when he came to London.

William Edin of Wallton in the cowntie of Buckingham-shieare a carpenter or plow wright being a single man who coming up to westminster hall and being there in sute of lawe took some inward griefe whereof he fell sicke and being lodged at the howse of william brooke a skinner being his kindsman and dwellinge at the signe of the cocke in hownsditche wheare he let [departed] his lyfe . . . yeares xxij. [1 June 1592]

Margaret Russell wyfe to Charles Russell cittizen and armeror of London dwelling neare the signe of the kinges head without Aldgate was buried the xxiiij[th] day of

24. Cf. "Take no thought for your life," "Take therefore no thought for the morrow" (Matt. 6:25, 31, 34, etc.) of the contemporary King James version of the Bible. See also Murray 1888; Wright 1857.

Januarie Anno 1593 yeares lx. who before had beine tempted with an evell speritt and nowe dyed of a thowght as by ye crowners quest [coroner's inquest] was soposed [believed].

To have "beine tempted with an evell speritt" was probably the popular explanation for the irrational behavior of the unfortunate woman. The fact that an inquest was held suggests that the circumstances of death were considered suspicious. Inquests will be discussed in a later chapter.

A man aged forty died "of a thowght having had long sute in Lawe" (4 June 1597), and a woman of thirty perished similarly, "hir husband being in prison" (24 December 1598 —Christmas Eve). There was a burial on 20 September 1623 of "a poore child kept [maintained] by the Inhabitants of Eastsmithfield. . . . The mother kept in Bedlem." "Bedlem" was the notorious London institution for the insane. A final instance was that of a man thirty-four "he dyed in the striete . . . of a frennezye" (29 April 1597). The brief entries have lost none of their tragedy in nearly four centuries.

V: "This Mortality of Pestilence"

Sickness could strike the people of London in many ways, none more terrible than when the diseases called plague crept out of hiding to rage about the streets and alleys. Plague was originally a nonspecific term, referring to any illness that swept people into their graves suddenly and in great numbers. The Black Death that spread horror over Asia and Europe in the fourteenth century was at least partly bubonic plague. The mortality from it in some European countries is thought to have been as much as three-fourths of the population; the death rate was even greater in England. Some of the early epidemics of "plague" may have been typhus or other rapidly spreading and lethal diseases. The great epidemics in Britain in the sixteenth and seventeenth centuries are believed to have been at least primarily bubonic plague. The disease had arrived in England by 1348 (Shrewsbury 1970), and was endemic from that date to 1665. It flared up periodically—in the sixteenth and seventeenth centuries in 1563, 1592–93, 1603, 1625, and 1665—the last outbreak being referred to as the Great Plague.[1]

Bubonic plague, the most frequent form of the disease, is spread from man to man by the bites of infected fleas, which are harbored by rats and other animals. The buboes that give this variety of plague its name are the characteristic infected, swollen, painful lymph nodes, particularly in the groin and armpits. Susceptibility to plague does not depend on sex, age, race, or occupation. The incubation period is likely to be from two to eight days. The death rate in the absence of effective treatment varies from 60 to 90 percent. There have also been some severe epidemics of pneumonic plague, passed from one victim to the next by droplets produced by coughing or expectoration. The incubation period of the pneumonic form is up to three days. The spread of either type of plague of course is greatly facilitated by overcrowded living conditions, lack of sanitation, and rat infestation (Mackie, Hunter, and Worth 1954; Manson-Bahr 1966).

Plague is a "disease of towns" and of poverty. Overcrowding and dirt favor the multiplication of rats, their close proximity to man, and the transfer of infected fleas. The epidemics from 1563 on have been correlated with

1. Mullett 1956; Payne 1937; Roberts 1966.

London's conspicuously enlarging population and its consequent physical growth (Roberts 1966).

The old women searchers described in chapter 3 of course were expected to report deaths from plague. Physicians usually abandoned the stricken unless they were wealthy. Thomas Lodge, himself a doctor, wrote during the epidemic of 1603:

> For where the infection most rageth there pouertie raigneth among the Commons, which hauing no supplies to satisfie the greedie desire of those that should attend them, are for the most part left desolate & die without reliefe.

Procedures ranging from quarantine to the wearing of charms were employed to try to check the spread of an epidemic of plague. During a minor epidemic in 1569 in London, the Lord Mayor and aldermen issued orders to constables, householders, and others "for preventing its spreading." The orders included:

> *Two Vewers of* DEAD BODIES.
> *Two Vewers of SICK-SUSPECTED shall*
> *be appointed and sworne.*

These Vewers to report to the Constable, he to the Clarke, and he to the Chiefe of Clarke. All upon Pain of Imprisonment. A Paine of standing on the Pillory[e] for false Reports by the Vewers. A Loss of Pension to such as shall refuse. [Maitland, 1756]

A few years later the regulations were reaffirmed (Wilson 1927). They were received at St. Botolph's on 23 February 1583.

> Memerandum of a precept From ye Lorde Maior concerninge ye avoidinge ye Infection of ye plague was read by M^r heayse [Hayes] in ye church.

The viewers were obliged to take an oath to report any cases of infection to the authorities, who were then supposed to establish a quarantine. The viewers, like the searchers of dead bodies, were ignorant old women. It appears that, in spite of penalties for making false reports or for neglect, they often transgressed. The job was disagreeable and dangerous. Like the searchers, the viewers were said to be highly susceptible to bribes. Even if they were honest they could make mistakes, since the visible signs of plague were variable and in the pneumonic form could be almost nonexistent. Birch, discussing this problem in 1759, concluded that

> we must suppose, that the true plague very often passed under the name of the spotted fever[2] This might be done willfully by some, who were unwilling to own, that the plague was in their houses; which is worth the attention of the magistrate. It probably sometimes happened by a mistake through ignorance; purples only appearing in several, who had the plague, without any buboes or car-

2. Probably typhus. Neither term appears in the St. Botolph records.

buncles; which is worth the attention of physicians. But, however it happened, we must conclude, that great as the reputed number was of those, who died of the plague, the real number was still greater.

In a footnote Birch quotes a letter of 14 September 1665 from one John Tillison to Dr. Sancroft, then Dean of St. Paul's Cathedral and later Archbishop of Canterbury. The letter, which Birch says is in the British Museum, volume 3785, among the papers of the Archbishop, reports that

> the practitioners in physic . . . stand amazed to meet with so many various symptoms, which they find among their patients (who are ill of the plague). One week the general distempers are blotches and boils; the next week are clear-skinned as may be. But death spares neither. One week full of spots and tokens, and perhaps the succeeding bill [of mortality] none at all.

Not only could there be confusion about diagnosis, but householders might do their best to deceive the viewers, primarily because of the limitations that would be imposed by the quarantine of a house for plague.[3] Also, to admit the

3. See *Romeo and Juliet* (act V, scene 2) for an instance of quarantine based on the report of searchers (Murray 1888; Wilson 1927). Quarantine involved strict confinement to a house marked with a cross and the legend "Lord have mercy on us." All the doors and windows were kept closed, and a watchman stood by. Elizabeth ordered a gallows to be erected at Windsor for the execution of any person who concealed a case of plague (Creighton 1902).

viewers to such a home would give them ample opportunity to collect gossip. Servants sick with plague were sometimes driven out without mercy, to die later on the street or in a barn. On occasion dead bodies would be carried off and left at a distance so that sickness would not be traced to a household. Or the sexton would be bribed to dispose of a body in another parish.[4]

Clearly, then, the plague statistics in the bills of mortality are not reliable. The true totals were probably considerably higher. Graunt (1759) estimated that "in the years of plague, a quarter part more dies of that disease than are set down." Mullett (1956) felt that only about two-thirds of the plague deaths were reported.

We cannot, of course, determine the degree of error in reporting plague deaths in the Parish of St. Botolph without Aldgate. There seems to have been no reason to report a death as having been caused by plague when some other cause was thought responsible. However, the reverse may have been true; some actual plague deaths may have been ascribed to other sicknesses, whether by honest error or deliberate deception. All this means that the reported parish death totals for this scourge, terrible though they were, may in reality have been too low.

The first plague epidemic of Elizabeth's reign struck in

4. Christie 1893; Creighton 1891, 1902; Mullett 1956; Wilson 1927.

1563. John Stow (1525?–1605), the great English chronicler, tells how it came.

> As ye have heard the plague of pestilence being in the towne of Newhaven,[5] through the number of souldiers that returned from thence into England, the infection thereof spread into divers parts of this Realme, but especially the City of London was so infected, that in the same whole yeere, that is to say, from the first of Jan. 1562 till the last of Decem. 1563[6] there dyed in the citie and liberties thereof containing 108 parishes of all diseases, 20.M.3.C.72 [20,372] and of the plague, (being part of the number aforesaid) 17.M.4.C.4 [17,404] persons.

If the eleven parishes outside the city (St. Botolph's was one of them) were included, 23,660 persons died in the twelve-month period, 20,136 of them of the plague, according to Stow (1631).

Supposed causes of death were not set down in the St. Botolph record books in 1563, but the plague makes itself evident in the abrupt rise in burials (table 1, fig. 3). There is a notation for July: "In this monethe the plauge began." As with other epidemics of the disease, its greatest severity was in the summer, although it did not burn itself out until December. The total burials for the period July through December 1563 were 573, as compared to 64 and 35 for the

5. A seaport on the English Channel.
6. That is, in one year.

corresponding periods in 1562 and 1564, respectively. Succeeding epidemics were to be much worse.

The parish records give detailed information on the epidemic of 1593. That year 1,463 people were buried in St. Botolph's churchyard—1,078, 73.7 percent, of them dead of plague, according to the record. Birch (1759) reproduces a bill of mortality "for the Year 1593." It is implied, but not stated, that this means the period from 21 December 1592 until 20 December 1593. In any case, its totals for the Parish of St. Botolph without Aldgate are wildly erroneous, showing 1,771 burials, 624 of them for plague deaths. Thus the bill overstated the total burials and understated the plague deaths.

Table 9 indicates the reported incidence of plague from 1585 to 1597 by month. No plague deaths were recorded in 1598, 1599, and the first five months of 1600, when notations as to cause of death ended. It is clear that the epidemic of "1593" actually broke out in August of 1592.

In figure 4 the large number of nonplague deaths of infants under the age of seven months is conspicuous, but, as was pointed out in chapter 3, a high mortality rate was characteristic of this age group. No deaths of chrisoms from plague were reported. Very striking is the concentration of most of the plague deaths in the under-forty age groups. The increase in the number of deaths in successive age groups is due mostly to the fact that the span of the age groups is longer and longer—five months, one year, two years, three

Table 9. Plague Deaths by Month, 1585–97

	1585	1586	1587	1588	1589	1590	1591	1592	1593	1594	1595	1596	1597
Jan.	1								7	6			
Feb.									2	1			
Mar.									11	4			2
April	1				1				32				3
May		1							48				1
June									59	2			1
July									152	2	1		1
Aug.								4	379			2	
Sept.	1							5	260		1	1	
Oct.								13	81			1	
Nov.			1					12	34	1			1
Dec.			1					4	13			1	
Total	3	1	2	0	1	0	0	38	1,078	16	2	5	9

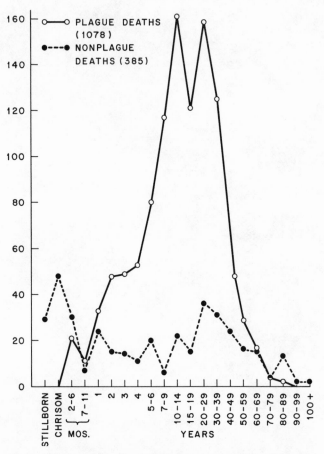

Fig. 4. Deaths and nonplague deaths by age groups, 1593. Note that age groups are not uniform, covering periods ranging from five months to ten years.

years, five years. The relatively small number of deaths after age thirty-nine might be explained on at least two bases. First, the death rate even in a normal year seems to have been high enough so that relatively large numbers of people could scarcely have lived to middle age. Second, those few persons who survived attacks of plague in the previous (1563) epidemic may have acquired immunity.

Figure 5 shows plague deaths only, by age group and by sex. The counts for males and females are similar into the ten-to-fourteen age group and then separate abruptly; the totals for females decline steadily while those for males continue to climb to a high for the twenty- to twenty-nine-year-olds. Then there is a precipitous drop, and by ages fifty to fifty-nine the curves for males and females again nearly coincide.

It is possible that there were many more plague deaths in the age groups five to forty-nine simply because a large part of the parish population belonged to these groups. We know from Graunt (1759) and others that London received a large, steady inflow of migrants from the country. They came not for the city's charms, a poor exchange for life in rural surroundings, but because they were hungry and looking for work. Older children were regularly employed in the sixteenth century, usually as servants and apprentices. The age groups showing the greatest losses due to plague were also the most employable. If this hypothesis were accepted, one would have to postulate that after age fourteen

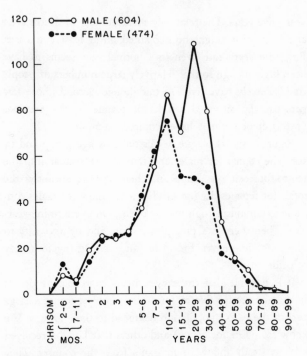

Fig. 5. Burials, plague victims only, by sex and age group, 1593.

the majority of the migrants were male. If all nonplague deaths in 1593 are now plotted by sex and age group (fig. 6), we note that the greatest male-female differences occur at ages one, twenty to twenty-nine, thirty to thirty-nine, and forty to forty-nine. I cannot account for the difference at age one. The conspicuous sex difference at ages twenty to forty-

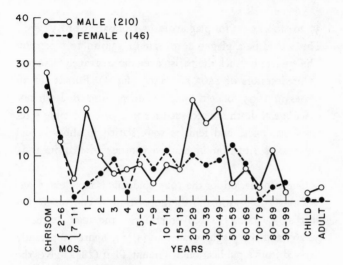

Fig. 6. Burials of nonplague victims by sex and age group, 1593. Compare with figs. 4 and 5.

nine in figure 6 overlaps but does not coincide with the period of male preponderance (ages fifteen to forty-nine) in figure 5. So figure 6, revealing that considerably more males than females of ages twenty to forty-nine died in 1593 from all causes other than plague, would seem to give limited support to the hypothesis that in the population at risk in this age range the males were considerably more numerous.

A plague epidemic broke out in London again in 1603. Mullett (1956) puts the city's total population in that year at 225,000. Estimates of deaths from all causes range from

37,294 to 42,042; for plague deaths, from 30,561 to 36,269.[7] This would be a plague death rate of 13.6 to 16.1 percent. The epidemic struck the parish even more savagely than had its predecessors of 1563 and 1593 (fig. 3). Burials for all causes in 1603 totaled 1,948. Neither cause of death nor exact age at death are recorded for that year, but table 5 reveals that males and females were buried in almost equal numbers, a situation in marked contrast to that in 1593 (fig. 5).

Our information for the 1625 epidemic is more extensive. Wilson (1927) estimates the population of London in that year at 320,000. He and others[8] put the total deaths at 54,265 and the plague deaths at 35,417, figures apparently derived from a publication by Graunt. Platt (1844) gives the total deaths as 51,758. He refers to the comments on the plague by Sir William Petty (1623–87), a British political economist.

> In pestilential years (which are one in 20), there dye [in London] ⅙th of the people of the plague and ⅕th of all diseases....
>
> Poor people who live close, dye most of the plague. The Plague is about 3 monthes rising and as much falling, which cold weather hastens. [Lansdowne 1927]

Wilson (1927) points out that the proportion of the population that died was even greater, for many residents of Lon-

7. Angus 1854; Birch 1759; Mullett 1956; Platt 1844.
8. Angus 1854; Mullett 1956; Walford, 1878.

don had moved temporarily to the country to escape contagion. This was the flight of the well-to-do and, too often,
of the medical profession. The poor had little choice other
than to stay behind and hope (Creighton 1902; Roberts
1966). But there was not much hope. The memories of
earlier epidemics must have been still vivid in the minds of
those who had survived them. Some would recall the despair
of Thomas Nashe (1567–1601) when he wrote *In Time of
Pestilence* in 1593.

> Adieu, farewell earth's bliss!
> This world uncertain is:
> Fond are life's lustful joys,
> Death proves them all but toys.
> None from his darts can fly;
> I am sick, I must die — —
> *Lord, have mercy on us!*
>
> Rich men, trust not in wealth,
> Gold cannot buy you health;
> Physic himself must fade;
> All things to end are made;
> The plague full swift goes by;
> I am sick, I must die — —
> *Lord, have mercy on us!*
>
> . . . .
>
> Strength stoops unto the grave,
> Worms feed on Hector brave;

> Swords may not fight with fate;
> Earth still holds ope her gate;
> *Come, come!* the bells do cry;
> I am sick, I must die — —
> *Lord, have mercy on us.*

The epidemic of 1625 began in St Botolph's parish with the burial of a single plague victim on 6 April. There was another death ten days later, and others followed, but only at the rate of one, two, or three a day, and only on some days. Nevertheless, the worried parish clerk knew the signs of coming disaster. Recording on 23 April the burial of the fifth person dead of plague, he added an earnest prayer, "Lord cease this sicknes." The next day he noted, "Three Birdes were killed with one Bolte"; the lethal stroke of lightning was an evil omen. Up to 7 June there were only 47 burials. Ninety-five more persons succumbed to plague as the death rate slowly accelerated. By then the people of the city knew that the horror was once again upon them. The clerk noted on 2 July that "the Generall Fast began this day In London." Plague fatalities were not regularly recorded as such at that time, but the ultimate death toll for all causes in the parish in 1625 was 2,479.

Curiously enough, this total represented 1,324 males and 1,155 females (table 5), a ratio of 114.6 to 100. In the epidemic of 1593 there were 604 male and 474 female deaths from plague in the parish (fig. 5), a ratio of 127.4 to 100.

We know that again in the 1625 epidemic males predominated in both the "Child" and "Adult" groups (table 5), but we do not know why.

The bill of mortality reproduced by Birch (1759) shows that for the period 16 December 1624 to 15 December 1625 there were 2,573 burials, 1,653 those of plague victims, in the Parish of St. Botolph without Aldgate. In this case the bill's total is somewhat closer to my count than it was for the year 1593.

The epidemic of 1625 was more severe for the parish and for London than those of 1563, 1593, and 1603. But it must be remembered that the population of the city was also growing rapidly, so that the numbers of people at risk were increasing steadily. In 1636 there was a lesser epidemic, and finally in 1665 the Great Plague struck its terrible blow, killing an estimated 68,596 people (Hirst 1953).

VI: Deaths by Accident and Violence

Not all deaths resulted from disease. A fall from a church steeple, a drunken quarrel in a tavern, the overturning of a small boat on the swift Thames—all could end fatally. Many such occurrences appear in the St. Botolph records, some as entries marking the burial of the victim and some as accounts of "crowner's quests."

The office of crowner, or coroner, is an ancient one in England, going back perhaps to Norman times (Waldo 1910). Originally the title of this officer was *custos placitorum coronae,* guardian of the crown's pleas or rights of private property. In practice, this meant that he looked out for the special profits due to the king. The royal fringe benefits included such items as hidden or sunken treasure that had been recovered and for which there was no owner, and also whales and sturgeons. Both creatures were "royal fish," considered the property of the king, and apparently much favored by connoisseurs. (The whale, esteemed by the crown or not, of course is a mammal.) The coroner was concerned with sudden death because when it was the result of murder, the property of the criminal was forfeited and a share went to the crown. Thus, "the concern of the Coroner was rather to bring the goods and chattels of the felon himself to justice" (Wellington 1905).

The coroner, who served for life if he performed his duties satisfactorily, gradually became an important peace officer. When death occurred under suspicious circumstances, it was his duty to call together a panel or jury of twelve local men[1] to hold an inquiry or inquest into the circumstances (Murray 1888; Wellington 1905). Before 1509 the law specified that

a Coroner shall have for his fee upon every inquisition taken upon the view of the body slain and murdered thirteen shillings and fourpence of the goods and chattels of him that is the slayer or murderer. [1 Hen. 8, cap. 7]

Eventually it became evident that coroners were refusing to do their duty:

1. The number was supposed to be twelve, but actually varied. For 1 May 1595 the St. Botolph record lists seventeen "names of them that weare of the foresayd Crowners quest Being parishioners Inhabiting within the ward."

> If any person hath happened to be slain by misadventure and not by no man's hand that they [the coroners] will not enquire upon the view of the body so by misadventure slain except they have for their labour thirteen shillings and fourpence. . . .

In other words, if someone died by accident, there was no murderer whose goods and chattels could be seized and hence no source for the coroner's fee. So the coroner refused to take action. To remedy this sorry state of affairs a law (1 Hen. 8, cap. 7) was passed in 1509–10 ordaining

> that upon a request made to a Coroner to come and inquire upon the view of any person slain drowned or otherwise dead by misadventure, the said Coroner shall diligently do his office upon the view of the body of every such person or persons without anything taking.

Only two coroners are mentioned by name in the St. Botolph parish records. There are references in 1588 and 1589 to a Master William Sawyer and again to a "Mr Squyer, coroner for the Cittie." In view of the permutations of Elizabethan spelling and of the fact that the two citations occur within less than a year, we can suppose that both names probably designate the same man. He was succeeded by Thomas Wilbraham, "crowner for the cittie of London," whose name appears fairly frequently from 23 June 1590 to 10 May 1600. There is for this last date a cryptic entry regarding Master Wilbraham. It seems that he did pannell a crowners quest in the parish church of St Buttolphes w^thout aldgate London on Satterday being the 10th day of May Anno 1600 in the Afternoone for that he was hurt in the Left Legg w^t a butchers sett being throwne at him in white chaple parish.

Here the entry ends. The dictionary gives numerous meanings for "sett." Among the throwable items are various tools and a granite paving block. Anyway, it sounds as though somebody in Whitechapel did not like Master Wilbraham. I have encountered no other instance in the records of a coroner's inquest into a case of nonfatal assault. It is understandable that the clerk, recording an attack on this exalted personage, should stick discreetly to the bare facts of the case, but it is too bad he could not tell us more. Why, for example, was the inquest not called in the parish where the incident occurred?

Now let us turn to an examination of the 111 accidental and violent deaths recorded from 1573 through 1624 in the parish. I have classified them as accidents, murder and manslaughter, executions, and suicides. Because of insufficient information, some deaths have had to be categorized rather arbitrarily, for example, when it was not clear whether the cause of death was accident or manslaughter.[2] In other instances the report is quite detailed. I shall try to let the facts that are reported speak for themselves. There is record

2. Homicide without malice expressed or intended.

of an inquest in 39 of the 111 deaths. Additional inquests may have gone unnoted.

Of the 55 deaths considered to be accidental, the commonest variety was drowning. There were 21 cases. The youngest was a boy of two, "by chance Drowned in a ditch" (8 December 1591).[3] A three-year-old girl died when a chair in a privy "whelmed backward" and she fell into the Town Ditch (13 October 1596). Joan Mallet, another youngster and daughter of a haberdasher,

> being a lone by itselfe playeng in the gray hound aley
> neare a shallow well of a garden . . . wheare by channce
> the said chyld fallling into the well was drowned and the
> crowners quest having seene and vewed the sayd chyld she
> was buried the xiij[th] Day of June ano 1592 yeares iij.

A question of negligence is implied in a rather similar accident.

> Memorandum that M[r] Thomas Wilbraham being the
> crowner for the cittie of London did pannell a crowners
> quest in the parish church of S[t] Buttolphs without Aldgate
> London on Thursday being the xxxj[st] day of August 1598
> to vewe the bodie of one Margaret Eldrington the daughter
> of Thomas Eldrington cittizen & gowldsmith of London

---

3. A good many deaths occurred at times when the age of the deceased was not recorded. I have classified such individuals as "Child" or "Adult" on the basis of the information available.

collexion for
reliebe sarten
ck people in
e prish as.
so to reliebe
boye borne
the pishe
hose ___ toes
eare rotted
f and ded
e in thecadge
s.

memerandom that a collexion was gatherd
in ower pishe churche By the churchwardens
the v:t Daye of marche in ano 1586
and was to reliebe sarten sicke psons
Dwellinge in the prishe weich wwas
in grtatt nede of Reliebe as also it
was to reliebe a poore Boye w:ch at this
Justant tyme ded lye in the towne so so
as it apeared, had bene some tonnesatd
and was Borne in this pishe abowght
x:vj ydards agone and are nowe his
fote weare Rotted of . and it was throwgt
he moste cost one of his fete / So that he
pishe ded strue to gett them in to the
hospitall   memorandum that after the
collexion Beinge endid m:r Deantes ded
sende vnto me ij:s to be Destributed to the
sicke the w:ch mony By the consent of
han gode all the churgwarden & Deh tid
vnto the goodman ___ the the tawman to
reliebe them in this sicknes the sayde daye

Richard Wilkinson the sonu of ___

April Anno 1590

the day
to 41.

Memorandum

Received of Richard ...
20 — shillings ...

3 . 7 . 5

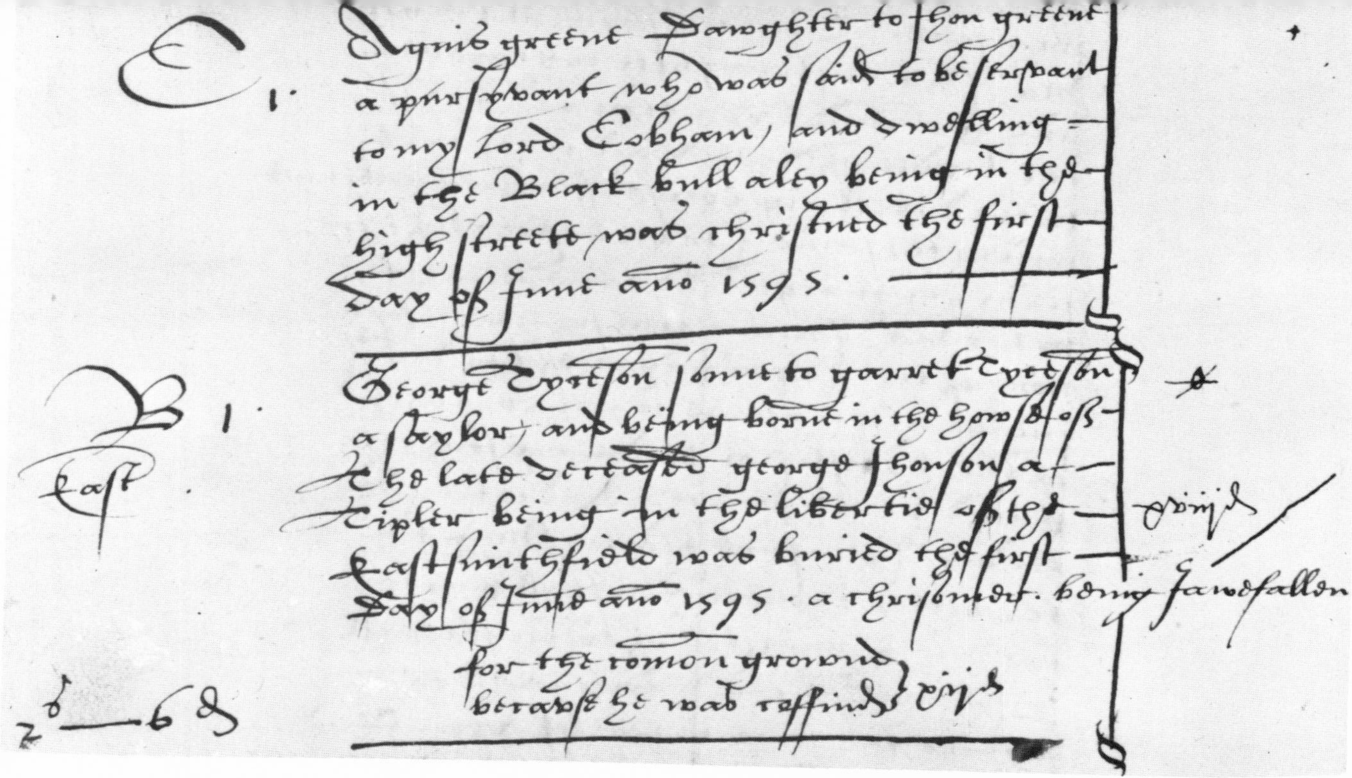

Fig. 9. Entries for a christening ("C") and a burial ("B"), 1 June 1595. The latter entry begins, "George Tyceson sonne to garret Tyceson a saylor and being borne in the house of the late deceased george Jhonson. . . ."

November Anno 1595

William Johannes sonne to ffraunces Johannes
20 Cittizen & haberdasher of London being a
Beare brewer & dwelling in the house of the
late deceased Anthony Dowsfild being
in the libertie of Eastsmithfeild was
Buried under his Dowsfilds stone being
at the sowth Andyed dore in the sowth
yle in the church clore by mr Dowsfild
the xx th day of November anno
1595 yeares iij

His funerall Chargis

ffor the minister ——————————— iij d
ffor the afternoones knell in the
greate bell ——————————
ffor the ground in the Church
ffor the best cloth not used
having a black cloth ———
ffor breaking the ground
in the Church ———
ffor the pealle ——————— ij d
ffor the pitts knell the
corps being coffind ———
ffor the clerkes attendance —

Fig. 10. William Johannes, son of well-to-do parents, had a relatively elaborate burial ceremony on 20 November 1595. The itemized list of charges begins with "ijd" (2d.) for the minister.

Fig. 11. Notations in connection with this burial on 31 January 1595 reveal the characteristically detailed knowledge of what went on in the parish.

the day.

31

Walter Goulden et al.

William Goulden

the 10 day of July
Anno 1595 the
wife of the

sonne and the

Saul Marie tayler

May Anno 1617.

B | Thomas Morton of Bounditch sure of the Stationers was buried the first and twentith day of May, Anno Dm 1617, in our Church whoe had a knell with the great Bell, and the Black Cloth, &c. } parish — xxij d m p

24 Maij 1617.

B | John Haley sonne to Matthew and Elizabeth Haley of East Smithfield was buried the xxiiijth day of May, Anno Dm 1617 an Infant. } 8

24 Maij 1617.

B | Peeter Gidding sonne to Thomas and Jane Gidding in the Highstreat was buried the xxiiijth day of May Anno Dm 1617 coffined in Mans Burying } parish — ijs iijd a Child.

25 Maij 1617

A Comunion. | On Sunday the xxvth day of his Month, the Holie Comunion was Ministred in our Church, at which time there was solde two gallons of wine, and iijs iiijd in Bread, the wine was had at the Swine Head, &c. } T. G.

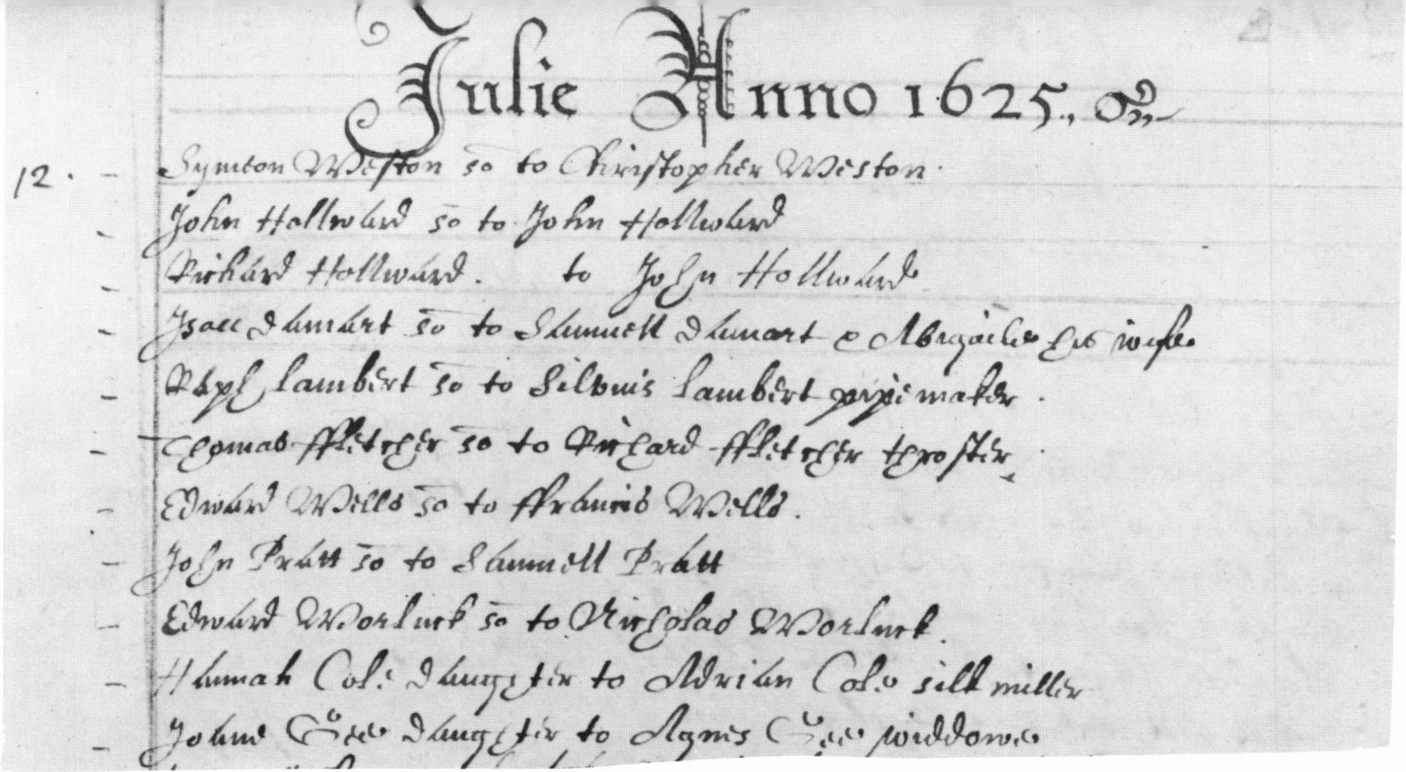

Julie Anno 1625, &c.

Symon Whetston so to Christopher Weston.

John Holward so to John Holward.

Richard Holward to John Holward.

Isaac Skinart so to Skinart Skinart & Abigaile his wife.

Rdof Lambert so to Gilbert Lambert gardinar.

Thomas Ayliffe so to Richard Ayliffe taylor.

David White so to Richard White.

John Pratt so to Samuell Pratt.

Edward Whorlwood so to Winefred Whorlwood.

Thomas Cole daughter to Abraham Cole silk miller.

John Gore daughter to Agnes Gore widdow.

12 —

Fig. 13. Brief, burried records of deaths during the great plague epidemic of 1625. All of these burials were on 12 July.

LORD HAVE MERCY UPON US.

This is the humble Petition of *England* unto Almighty God, meekely imploring his Divine bounty for the cessation of this Mortality of Pestilence now raigning amongst us : With a lamentable List of Deaths Triumphs in the weekly Burials of the City of LONDON, and the Parishes adjacent to the same.

LORD SHew thy pity on this sinfull Land,
Have We not felt enough thy heavy hand:
Mercy We beg of thee, doe not sweete God
Vpon Thy people too long lay thy Rod,
Vs In thine anger doe not quite consume,

Have We so wicked been, that thou canst not
Mercy Afford ? O is thy wrath so hot
Vpon Us that it can't be quench'd with teares?
Vs Thou hast spar'd (indeed) for many yeares,
LORD We confesse it, yet on our repentance,

An exact and true relation of the number of those that were buried in London and the Liberties of all diseases, from the 17. of March 1592. to 21. of December, 1593.

	totall.	Pl.
March 17	351	31
March 24	219	29
March 31	307	27
April 7	203	33
April 14	290	37
April 21	310	41
April 28	350	29
May 5	339	38
May 12	300	42
May 19	450	58
May 26	410	61
June 2	441	81
June 9	399	99
June 16	401	108
June 23	850	118
June 30	1440	927
July 7	1510	893
July 14	1491	958
July 21	1507	922
July 28	1503	283
August 4	1501	797
August 11	1532	651
August 18	1508	449
August 25	1490	507
Septemb 1	1210	563
Septemb 8	621	451
Septemb 15	629	349
Septemb 21	450	330
Septem 29	403	387
Octob. 6	432	345

1625.	totall.	Pl.
March 17	161	4
March 24	216	8
March 31	243	11
April 7	239	10
April 14	256	24
April 21		

1630.	totall.	Pl.
June 24	205	19
July 1	209	25
July 8	317	42
July 15	350	50
July 22	229	49
July 29	779	77
August 5	210	70
August 12	146	65
August 19	169	54
August 26	170	67
Septemb. 2	330	66
S. Fram 9	269	63
Septem 16	264	68
Septem 23	174	57
Septem 30	269	56
Octob. 7	236	65
Octob. 14	261	73
Octob. 21	248	62
Octob. 28	214	34
Novemb. 4	242	39
Nov. 11	215	19
Nov. 18	210	18
Nov. 25	226	7
Decemb. 2	211	22
Decemb. 9	158	29
Decemb. 16	212	5

The true number of all that dyed of overall diseases, Anno 1630. or thereabouts, are here lower and truly riseth, and summed up, though a little later beginning as followeth, and to learne howe she did com by hir death. At wch tyme it was certified before the sayd crowner and quest that the sayd Margaret Eldrington being a chyld abowt the age of Fyve yeares was playing with other smale children on wednesday the xxx^th day of august ano 1598 in the yeard of Mr Thomas Goodman gen[tleman] neare a pond in the said yeard. being in the said parish where the said Margaret fell in the said pond neare a stable end and with the water of the said pond the said Margaret was choked and drowned whereof she dyed wch pond lying open neare the sayd stable was verie dangerous for children, wherefore it was presented by the said crowners quest.

A boy aged seven or eight "was drowned in Goodmans Feilds in a Pond, playing with other Boyes there and swymming" (19 May 1615). Small children lost their lives "in a ditch in pond alley" (10 February 1612) and even "in a Tubb of water" (27 July 1614; 21 December 1618). A fourteen-year-old girl "drowned in a pond behynd her fathers howse . . . by mischance fetching a payle of water" (17 December 1597). A woman of twenty-two had a similar accident,

> beinge by chawnce Drowned in the Towne Ditche near the said garden stayere [stair] fetchinge of water the xxvij^th Day of August ano 1598 being one a tewsdaye at nyght aboute the ower of viij or nyne of ye clocke. [31 August 1598]

It is, incidentally, a measure of the sanitation, or lack of sanitation, of the times that the same Town Ditch that supplied water for domestic use also served the privies (see above).

Drownings in the nearby Thames were not uncommon. On 28 June 1591 a bargeman, aged twenty-six, was "washinge himselfe in the River of the Theames where the streame [current] taking him he was drowned." A cooper who was working on a lighter transporting beer from a wharf to a ship in the Pool of London died when he fell into the river "neare Lymehouse" (23 May 1590). Another disaster involved the deaths of several people in December 1616. One of them, Joan Moorton, wife of a sailor, was buried 21 January.

> Shee (with divers others) was by great Misfortune drowned in the River of Thames . . . coming by water from Wanseworth[4] and not found till this time, The Lord deliver us from such like Mischance, for God knoweth, it was a sorowfull voyage to them.

Falls, ten in number, were the second most frequent cause of accidental death. A six-month-old boy fell from a window; a sixty-two-year-old man, from a horse (30 July 1593; 4 August 1593). Thomas Martin, son of a cooper and climbing where he probably was not supposed to be, "died of a Fall, from the Toppe of a Shippe" (2 December 1623). The remaining accidents of this type involved adults. In

4. Wandsworth, a district on the south bank of the Thames.

two cases there were no details (15 September 1619; 25 February 1622). The other five were occupational injuries; we can only surmise that the last of these was indeed a fall.

> A Crowners quest was panelled in ower parishe churche the second day of August 1589 by on Mr Squyer crowner for the Cittie and was to go upon Richard Hitchingson a carpenter who was killed beinge at worke neare leden stall.

The burial entry gives more information.

> Richard Hitchingson a howsholder being a carpenter . . . who dyed of a Fall in doctor pennye his howse beinge there at worke and the crowners quest havenge vewed hem they ded Fynd that he was exesorie [accessory, contributory] to his owne death he was xxvj yeares owld.

This is one of the few instances in which the finding of the inquest was reported. The idea may have been to relieve Doctor Penny of any suspicion of negligence.

> Derick van Veedar a straunger being the cooke of a shipp called the Samson of Emdon[5] he being vearing [veering, paying out] the sheat or sayle of the said shipp being in the Road before woollwich[6] fell from the mast in to the ship whereof he dyed & being browght from thence to the

5. Probably Emden, a German port on the North Sea.
6. Woolwich roadstead, a somewhat sheltered anchorage on the Thames, downstream from London.

howse of Henrie Jhonson a tayler dwelling neare the hollands [blotted and illegible] being in the libertie of Eastsmithfield where a crowners quest being panneled for the same & the said quest having vewed his body he was buried the ixth day of March Anno 1596. yeares xix he was a bacheler & was no parishioner w^t us.

John Midleton, in Ship Alley, who by a Fall from a scaffold caught his death. [8 April 1612]

Édward Frier, a Bricklayer who dwelt in the Minories street .... He died of a fall, which he had, from the topp of the new Church at Wapping, where he wrought. [3 November 1618]

Edward Ellyard, a Seafaring-man. ... he died of a hurt which hapned him on Shipbord, being sore brused. [7 June 1621]

Crushing injuries and blows from various inanimate objects caused six deaths.

Edward poll servant ... being killed wth a peece of tymber as he wrought in the Duke place wth in algat.[7] [7 December 1585]

Thomas Sallmon ... killed by ye fall of a milstone galyekye [Galley Quay]. [9 May 1587]

Richard Freland the sonne of Richard Freland a saylor dwelling beyond the minneries [Minories] who ryding

7. Duke's Place, a street just inside Aldgate.

behind in a carr [wagon] laden with too hoggsheads of shipp beefe of his fathers to be shipped at St Katherynes Docke the which carr being tourned to go backwards with the said beefe at the upper end of the said docke and the hoggsheads rowlinge backe ded breake the rope and one of the said hossgheads ded fall out of the said carr upon the said chyld. . . . yeares xiiij. [18 September 1592]

A woman, and hir Child, who by the fall of a house in Pond alley, were both Slaine . . . wee could not learne hir name. [2 July 1616]

Robert Leamon Labourer who Died with a Blow given him with a [lump of] Seacole. [5 July 1624]

The circumstances of this last fatality seem suspicious, but the record gives no details, and an inquest is not mentioned.

Five deaths were due to injuries given by one person to another. At least three of the deaths seem clearly to have been accidental.

Thomas priestman the sonne of cutbart priestman a Tunman[8] to Mr Anthony Dowffield a beard [beer] brewer. . . . This chyld playing in Mr Dowffelds yeard the xxjth day of may ano 1589 was spurned one [kicked on] the belly by a Boy about ye age of x yeares whose name was caled Jacke being masterles[9] and whose surname was not knowne. . . . The Foresayd chylde dyed and the crowners

8. One who handled tuns or barrels.
9. Masterless, not apprenticed.

quest havinge gone upon hem . . . the sayd chylde was Buried the xxiij Day of may ano 1589 years xj.

A man of twenty was "killed wth a pichfork." There are no further details (10 July 1593).

An inquest was held on 24 April 1594 on the death of Abraham Brewer, aged forty,

a seafaring man or gonner of a ship dwelling in garden aley being in the precinct neare [the] tower who being hurt upon the river of the thames with the strype [blow] of an ower [oar] on the head whereof he dyed.

By coincidence, there were two very similar accidents within a few days at fencing schools.

Averie Barwick a yeoman dwelling near St Bennett powles [Paul's] wharfe who being hurt in the eye at foyles in the Dukes [place] at A School of fence was lodged at the house of Myles Lanckester a cooke dwelling at the signe of the blue bell where he dyed. [27 January 1599]

Thomas Wilbraham, the coroner, held an inquest a week later following the death of

Robert Wharton servant to William Lodge a brewer dwelling at Stratford Bowe: who being hurt in the eye with a cudgell in a schoole of fence and lying at the howse of Robert Hurtlie an Inhowlder [innkeeper] at the signe of Three Noonnes [Nuns] in the high streete where he dyed. [3 February 1599]

Four small children died of burns, all in accidents at home (17 November 1594; 24 February 1596; 31 January 1617). Two of the tragedies occurred on the same day in different households; all could have been prevented.

Vehicular accidents fortunately were not the commonplace that they have become in the twentieth century, but a horse or cart caused four deaths that are cited in the St. Botolph record. A boy of two was "killed in a cart" on 21 July 1589. An inquest on another victim was held on 5 January 1595

> to take viewe of the Bodie of on Bridgett Serten a mayden being the daughter of Thomas Serten of copt hall greene in Essex and to learne how she did come to her death who was killed by chance with a carte neare Aldgate going in to London.[10]

The burial record indicates that Bridget, aged twelve, was caught by the cart "betwene the parculles[11] and the gate post."

Michael Barom, a child, was "Slaine with a Cart" on 6 November 1615.

Richard Staples "having a Tankard of water in [*sic*] his Shoulder a Horse-man Runne over him at Aldgate, and overthrew him, and was sore wounded in the head by the

10. That is, entering the City through the gate.
11. A portcullis was an iron grating that could be lowered to block a gateway.

horse, whereof he died" (16 September 1615). One can picture the congestion as pedestrians and the drivers of carts
and wagons, some trying to enter the City and others
struggling to leave it, contested for passage through the gate
in the wall.

Guns and gunpowder were relatively new in Elizabethan
England. Very little powder was manufactured there before
the 1560s; until then it had been imported from the Con-
tinent (Rowse 1951). So it is not surprising that gunpowder
caused accidents. Mention has already been made of the ex-
plosion of a small cannon during the firing of a salute (see
chap. 4). On 30 June 1588, the parish was called on to help

> one Frauncis smithe of the Borroughe of Sothworke in the
> countie of Surrye Saultpeter[12] maker who beinge in fleete
> lane in a goon poulder house [gunpowder factory] there
> to receive monye for sault peeter the sayde house by
> casualtie of fyer aboute fower yearse last past was Blowne
> up with goon poulder whereby he was greeviously Bourned
> Disfigured and maymed in Dyvers parts of his bodye
> aparant to be howld wherefore he hath bene a long tyme
> sicke and in great payne spendinge and concerninge all
> that ever he could make in sekinge helpe for to cure him
> selfe.

The naiveté of the city fathers regarding the newborn indus-
try is sufficiently revealed by the fact that a gunpowder fac-
tory was permitted on Fleet Lane, close to Fleet Street!

12. Saltpeter, potassium nitrate, is an ingredient of gunpowder.

Alms had to be provided by the parish on 21 September 1595 for

> Edward Chilton a goune maker . . . who about vj yeares last past lost his left hand trying of a peece cawled a muskett.

Some victims of accidents with guns and gunpowder did not escape with their lives. There was an inquest in the parish church

> to enquyer howe Richard Hawkesworth a single man being a shoomaker of Blacke fryers came to his end who was hurt by mischaunce in a may game[13] cominge thorowghe Aldersgate striete wth a pece [piece, gun] one [on] his necke and havinge serten powder in his slieve which by mischaunce he shooting of his sayd peece fyered the sayd powder hurte or burnt his arme and his syde wheare of he dyed he was hurt one hollye [holy] thersday or asention [Ascension] Day[14] and dyed not hentell [until] the xxiijth Day of June 1590 . . . 24 yeares.

Sleeves in those days could be full and made pockets convenient for many things including, apparently, gunpowder! The foolhardiness of this young man was matched by

William Robertson servant to Edward Parker Farrier[15]

---

13. A game around the maypole.
14. Forty days after Easter.
15. A blacksmith who shod horses.

... he was Slaine by heating an old Barrell of a peece in their forge which [barrel] was Charged [loaded] and flew in peeces. [4 June 1621]

Two accidental deaths were due to asphyxiation. "Henrye White A pumpmaker ... was smothered by the damp of a well" (14 July 1584), quite probably when he descended into the well to make repairs. The well was at a tavern, The Three Cranes, operated by one Mistress Bird in Thames Street very close to the river and the Tower. It is likely that "damp" (in this sense now an obsolete term except for gases such as carbon dioxide and methane that may accumulate in coal mines) had been produced by rotting vegetation near the water and had collected in the well. Such gases are odorless and give no warning; in sufficient concentration they can be fatal.

A pensioner died on 7 December 1620; "hir Chamber was on fire, and shee smothered with the smoke thereof."

Not all violent deaths, of course, were accidental. Before we consider the cases of homicide, mention may be made of an attempted murder, a death due to unknown cause, and a suspected abortion.

Elizabeth Asher, the Reputed daughter of Thomas Asher in Wollsack alley in hounsdish the Mother named Joane Tagge, Servant to Thomas Newton a Broker in hounsditch, who like a Murderous Strumpett, cast hir said Child into a Privie, but by Gods good grace it was heard to Cry by the Neighboures and saved a live and Christned the tenth day of May Anno 1615, shee [the mother] was taken afterwarde and Araigned but escaped death. The Poore Infant dyed within a fortnight after.

Joan Austin, a widow, was buried 21 August 1623; "there was a Coroners Enquest went upon hir because hir Death was Sodaine." Presumably, foul play was suspected.

Another inquest was held by Master Wilbraham, the coroner, in the parish church on 14 May 1591

to Inquyre howe a man chyld borne in the alye behynd Mᵣ Lawtins howse neare the gardens in the presinct of hownsdich came by his death which chyld was Borne of the body of Dorathy Medcalfe the wyfe of peter Medcalfe a lewd fellowe having no serten dwelling place the xiij Day of may ano 1591.

The mother claimed that the baby was stillborn, but the "Jurie quest" must have suspected a criminal abortion. Their verdict is not recorded.

Of thirty other cases, all were rather clearly homicides but not all were definitely murders. Inquests are mentioned in most cases. Stabbings with knife, dagger, rapier, and even shoemaker's awl caused twelve deaths.

Matthias Eggere a straunger beinge A Bachelor and beinge By his occupation a Barber surgion he was yᵉ surgion of a shipp called the Blacke Ravon of Emdon who beinge in the howse of Cane Jhonson a Drayman Kepinge a tiplinge howse[16] near the signe of Harlem.[17] . . . With one Jeoste Emkin also a straunger late cooke of the said shipp with whome he had some words and stryvenge togither was by chaunce pricked with a knyfe by the sayd Jeoste where of he dyed. And the crowners quest having taken sufficient vewe of hem he was Buried the xij[th] Day of Februarie Ano 1587 beinge no parishioner yeares xxv.

A marginal note adds, "channce medlye."[18]
Master William Sawyer, the crowner, called a jury

and Ded sweare them to give trewe evedence how Jhon Dunstone a Bricklayer Dwellinge at the Blewe Anker neare Sparrowes corner ded com by his Deathe [He] was killed on Wedensdaye at nyghte the 15th of Maye 1588 aboute the ower of eyght or nyne of the clocke sittinge on his seate at his Bord [board, table] by Thomas Campyon a Laboringe man who Thruste him into the Backe under the Leafte shoulder Blade w[t] a knyfe wheare of he Dyed presently.[19]

The burial notation adds that the wound "wente aboute v entchis Deepe into his Bodye and more." Campion was executed for this crime (see below).

16. A tavern.
17. The sign was that of the city of Haarlem in Holland. Many Dutch sailors came to the taverns.
18. Quarrel.
19. In Shakespeare's day "presently" meant immediately.

Evert Corin, skipper of the Dutch ship *George*

being jesting with one Lambert a Dutchman whose surname was not knowne and in the house of Moyses van
Dam a tipler Dwellinge at the sign of the haddocke in
the libertie of Eastsmithfield where by mischaunce the
sayd Lambert ded hurt him wth a knyfe whereof the
foresayd Evert dyed and the Crowners quest havinge
vewed hem he was Buried the vth Day of December ano
1589 beinge no parishioner yeares xx.

On 22 May 1590 the parish buried

a yonge man not beinge knowne with a smale Red Barde
[beard] being Brode vissiged [broad visaged] who was in
a brown canvass Dublett Beinge cutt havinge also on him
a whyt friese jerkin and an owld blake cloke with theewe[20]
holes on eatch syde who was killed with a knyfe by a
Dutchman neare swan alye gate in the libertie of eastsmithfield. The sayd Dutchman whose name was [blank
space] ded stabb a knyfe thorowe his Ryght arme neare
the upper part of his Bodye whereof he dyed. . . . he was
aboute the age of xxiiij yeares being no parishioner.

David Jones a welschman being servant to Mathyas Dutton
a beare brewer . . . being one of his tonn [tun] men and
coming owte of his master his Dore beinge in drynke was
there thrust thorowe the bellye with a sword abowte the

20. A thew was a lace or cord.

ower of ten of the clocke at nyght the xxiiij^th Day of may
ano 1591 as it was thowght by one George Aplebie a
saylor and dyed the next morninge. . . . he was about the
age of xxxix yeares.

Mark Symonds a saylor being a bachelor bourne in Sweth-
land who being drinking with Jhon [blank space] Peter
[blank space] Cornelius and Jacob Jhonson being hol-
landers and in the company of dyvers others of his owne
contrimen in the howse of Derick Wynen a tipler dwelling
at the signe of the prince . . . where he was thrust with a
poneyeard [poniard] into the body and also thrust into
the theygh with a rapier of the wch wounds he Dyed being
the vij^th Day of October ano 1592 . . . being about the age
of xxiij yeares.

Memorandum that a crowners quest was panneled in the
parishe church of St Buttolphes wth out Aldgate London
the xth day of June anno 1594 in the forenoone by M^r
Wilbram the crowner for the cittie and was to Inquire
owt how thomas pilgram a gardener ded com by his death
being thrust into the throte and so hurt whereof he dyed
. . . he ded dwell in the parish of St Saviors in southwarke.

Derick Martinson a shipwrygt belonging to a ship called
the hope of Rotterdam being a maryed man having a
wyfe and one chyld liveing & dwelling at Rotterdam in
holland being beyond the seas This said derick being hurt
in the said shipp . . . by one Jhon Cloysonne of the said

shipp who thrust him into the body with a knyfe. [23
December 1595]

This last victim was thought to be about forty years old. No
inquest is mentioned, perhaps because the knifing occurred
on board the ship.

Jhon Andliegen dwelling neare the signe of the Redd
Lyon being in the precinct as we go toward the Tower,
he was thrust into the bodie with his owne weapon by one
Thomas Taylor being one of the knyght Marshalls men[21]
within the howse at the Rose Taverne being near All-
hallowes Barking church whereof he dyed. [8 September
1596]

There is again no mention of an inquest.

William Clement a sayler whose dwelling was said to be
in Loo in Davonsheare who was thrust into the left syde
of his bodie under the pappes [pap, nipple] with a rapier
by one [blank space] Aldersie a sayler dwelling in an alley
being called Jennings Rentte . . . where he dyed. [20
January 1598]

Cornelius Johnson, a Saylor, slayne by one of his fellowes
in eastsmithfield with a knife, on Mr James Desmaistres
his wharf . . . a Dutchman. [19 November 1612]

Christopher Bodie servant to one John Townesend a Player

21. The knight marshal was an officer in the royal household
and was concerned with violations of the law there.

. . . was buried the fifteenth day of November, Anno Dni 1619. He was Stab'd by a drayman, with a Shoemakers All, and Dyed of that wound. The Coroners Enquest viewed the Corps before it was Buried.

It is noteworthy that in the twelve homicides at least four of the assailants and seven of the victims were sailors.

The cause of death was not specified in the records of eleven other killings.

Elizabeth skynner wedow dwelling at the corner-howse next unto hogg laynn end in the eastsmithfield was murthered in hir ownne howse & so found lying dead wth in hir entry. [20 January 1579]

Richard Todd was executed for this crime (see below).

On 1 August 1580 Robert Joonnis, servant of Thomas Jackson, was buried. He had been "murthered."

Ulisses monmouth servant unto Sir willm [William] knight who was slayne by one m^r candich Jentil [Gentleman] was buryed. [29 November 1582]

Thomas Jonnes servant to Mr James de Meatris[22] a Brewer dwelling at the signe of the shipp . . . who was murdered in the said howse as it is said by one of his fellowes . . . yeares xxx. —The Crowners quest had seene him Fynding

22. Presumably this was the same man on whose wharf Cornelius Johnson was murdered (see above).

him wilfully murdered by one of his fellowes. [26 December 1593]

Jhon Takle a wyne porter . . . he was kild. [29 December 1600]

Ellen Hunt and Alice Burnham were buried on 2 May 1609.

This Ellen Hunte and Alice hir Mayd were both Cruelly murthered By one Morgan Colman who lodged in hir House, 27 Aprill.

A woman Chyld, which was found Murthered, among Tymber in east smithfeild. [3 October 1611]

There is a record of the christening on 29 January 1614 of

Mary Rubee, daughter to Hester Rubee in hounsditch, whose husband named franciscus Rubee Silkthrowster (and an Italian) fled out of the land, for a Murder by him comitted on one M^r [blank space] his wives kinsman, at Montague house in Southwark.

John Powes servant to Roger Somerland victualer neere the Tower hill . . . he was slayne by the Tower Ditch . . . The Coroners Enquest viewed the bodie before it was buried. [3 July 1619]

William French Labourer of Gravell Lane (who was slayne by his owne Brother). [10 July 1619]

The grim procession of entries continues. The tyranny

of a master over his man is illustrated by the fact that the deaths of no less than three servants were suspected or known to be due to "misuse" by their employers. A coroner's inquest was called on 1 May 1595 to look into the death of Bridget Bayly, a woman of thirty who had worked for one Cuthbert Donne, a farrier. She was taken to the hospital, then moved to a private home, where she expired. The jury "viewed" the body "to Inquyre out whereof she dyed the rather for that it was said she was misused by her late M^r the said Cuthbart Donn his wyfe." The burial charge, 5s. 5d., "was payd by Mrs Dunn."

Thomas Ashton, whose age was not reported, was employed by Anthony Rowland, a cooper of East Smithfield. Ashton died on a Saturday. He was disinterred the following Monday, 30 August 1596, on orders of the coroner of Middlesex, the county in which London lay, and

> was viewed by a quest . . . for that speeches were given of him that his master had given him corection wch was said to have beene the occation of his death which was not proved.

Master Rowland paid the burial charges to the sexton.

Blame for the servants' deaths could not be fixed on these masters—and mistresses—but there was no doubt in a third case.

Susanne Poynard, servant to one Thomas Guest a Glover

in Rosemary lane, who dyed by sore beating of hir dame,[23] and the Coroner satt about the said busines, to fiend out by an Enquest how she came by hir death. [21 July 1613]

Both Thomas Guest and his wife were executed for causing the death of Susanne Poynard.

A little girl of six and another of thirteen were murdered by rapists (12 May 1587; 13 July 1594). The men responsible were identified, but there is no mention in the parish records of inquest or prosecution.

Two other homicides complete the list. A coroner's jury was sworn in the parish church on 10 April 1592

to vew the body of Marie Clarke the deare beloved wyfe of Mr George Clarke cittizen Vintner of London Who was soposed to dye of a blowe or strype given her on the face the Thursday was a sennite before[24] by one Roger Berkwith and that in her owne howse being at the signe of the kings head without algate.

The names of eighteen men are listed

who weare apoynted by the crowner to make there next meeting at the Guildhall before him on the wedensday in the whitson weeke[25] abowt the ower of one of ye clock.

23. The mistress of the household.
24. A week ago Thursday.
25. The week following Whitsunday, the seventh Sunday after Easter.

There is no further information in the record about this death, very likely because the inquest was held at the Guild-hall rather than in the parish.

A three-year-old girl, not the daughter of a parishioner, was "found strangled with a Fillet [band of cloth] in a hay-mowe" in a loft over the storehouse of a brewer. There was an inquest. Another entry for the preceding day, 26 March 1594, tells of the burial of a woman of about twenty-four who was found dead in the same hayloft. Her name "was not knowne and as it seemed was one that went a gooding,"[26] that is, she was a beggar. The body was viewed

> by william Lawdian the baylie [bailiff] . . . and william sanders and leonard fingerman constables . . . and also by the ij searchers who fynding that she dyed of a bleache she was buried.

Now the clerk is very careful not to speculate, but it seems reasonable for us after nearly four centuries to guess at what appears to have been a double tragedy. The homeless, starving, desperate mother may have taken the life of her daughter and then somehow destroyed herself. Examination by the bailiff and two constables as well as by a pair of searchers would have been most exceptional for a death due to "bleach" but not surprising if suicide was suspected. On the other hand, the latter was not mentioned officially. Such

26. This quaint term came from the practice of extending good wishes when alms were received.

an omission would be an act of charity, as it was both religious and superstitious practice to deal very harshly with
the remains of one who had killed herself (see below). So
there was no inquest, the searchers obligingly assigned an
acceptable "cause" of death, and the wretched mother's body
was laid in the churchyard after all.

The remains of no less than seventeen executed persons,
all but one of them men, were buried in the parish. This
number seems startlingly high until we remember that
capital punishment was a commonplace in the Tudor period
(Rowse 1951). The records lack full details, but it appears
that thirteen of the men were hanged for piracy at Execution Dock in Wapping, downstream from the Tower. Stow
says in his *Survey* (Thoms 1842) that this was "the usual
place of execution for hanging of pirates and sea rovers, at
the low-water mark, and there to remain, till three tides had
overflowed them." No doubt it was believed that sailors
passing on the Thames and seeing the busy gibbet would be
deterred from a life of crime. Piracy was not unusual as late
as the sixteenth century.

Thomas nicolson prisoner executed at wappinge was
buried. [25 April 1577]

Walter debarnell[27] saylor executed at wappinge. [4 April
1579]

Wa[l]ter Wren and Charles Wakam who were executed

27. Elsewhere in the record the name appears as Davernly.

at Waping for robing of a spanishe shipp in the straights were buryed in this our churchyard of me their confesso[r] curat here.[28] [8 July 1580]

Phillip boyl for pyracy on the seas was executed at Waping and in this church was buried. [21 July 1580]

Thomas waters servannt to samuel biggs a prisoner in the mshalsey [Marshalsea] was buryed. [11 July 1581]

The Marshalsea Prison was in Southwark, on the south side of the Thames. A marginal notation adds, "thomas waters executed at wapin." The notation gives us one reason for guessing that Waters's crime was piracy. Prisoners who had the funds, as Samuel Biggs apparently did, could hire other prisoners as their servants. The second reason for thinking that Waters was a pirate is that Biggs died for the same crime:

Samuell biggs a captain for piracy on the seas was executed at wapping & buryed in this church. [1 August 1581]

Perhaps Waters had been Captain Biggs's servant at sea as well.

The burial record continues:

Hewgh Knight a Sayller & executed at wapping was buried the 25 Daye off Julye. [1581]

Clinton Atkinson some tyme a howskp [housekeeper] &

28. The writer was Robert Hayes, the curate.

dwelling in grace church street & sold haberdash^e[ry] warr^s [wares] was for piracy executed at wapping. [31 August 1583]

Willm valentin yere /23/ executid. [31 August 1583]

Edmonnd coppinger a sailler a maryed man was for piracy executed & buryed. [31 August 1583]

Thomas Cowdall A maryner executed Att wappinge for piracye. [30 August 1587]

Thomas Edwards being a batchelor he was borne in Glossetere being a sea Faringe man and executed at wappinge For pyracy the xxx^th Daye of August in ano 1587 betwixt the ower of too and three of the clocke was Buried the sayde xxx^th Daye of August in ano 1587. beinge xxviij yeares owld no parishioner.

It is curious that except for two of the pirates who were hanged in April in 1577 and 1579, all of the others went to Execution Dock in the months of July or August. Perhaps trials for piracy were held only in the summer months.

The four remaining executions were for murders already described. Richard Todd, "gonner & householder," died at Tyburn[29] on 1 April 1580 for causing the death of Mistress Elizabeth Skinner. Thomas Campion, a laborer,

29. The public gallows there stood close to the present location of Marble Arch in Hyde Park.

for murderinge of Jhon Donstone a Bricklayer was executed ryght over agaynst the Signe of the Blewe Anker
near the highwaye that goth towarde Hogg Lane within
the Libertie of London the xxiij^th Daye of maye 1588.

Dunstone had been killed in the Blue Anchor (see above).
His murderer was hanged as close to the scene of the crime
as possible. Thomas Guest and his wife were executed
9 August 1613 at Tyburn, nineteen days after the murder
of their servant, Susan Poynard.

The parish records tell of one probable and six definite
suicides.

Agnis miller wieff of Jacob Miller who killed her selfe
wth a kniff was putt in the ground. [27 August 1573]

Note that the record says, "putt in the ground," not "buried."
This means that there was no burial service and that interment was not in a church or churchyard.

In 1590 a coroner's inquest was held in St. Botolph's
Church to investigate a suicide. The coroner, Master Thomas
Wilbraham, wished to

examen howe Amye Stokes the wyfe of Henrie Stokes a
sawyer Dwellinge in Jhon Ansell his yeard . . . Did com by
her death who hanged her selfe in her chamber beinge
over a sawpitt in the forenamed Mr Ansell his yeard the
seventh day of september ano 1590 abowte the ower of
ix of the clocke in the forenoone in manner and forme

followinge That is to saye she had cast a cord abowte a
beame in her sayd chamber Fastninge it to the sayd beame
and puttinge the same with slydinge knott abowte her
neck as it apeared standinge upon a three Footed stoole
wch with one of her feete she had thrust from her and so
hanged her selfe her feete standinge Bent upon the flower
or borde of the sayd chamber and being fownde by the
Jurie or Crowners quest that she Fallinge from god had
hanged or murthered her selfe, Where upon Judgment
was given . . . by the sayd crowner that she should be
carried from her sayd howse to some cross way neare the
townes end and theare that should ha[ve a] stake dreven
thorowgh her brest and so be buried with the stake to be
seene for a memoryall that others goinge by seeinge the
same myght take heede for comittinge the lyke faite. And
the sayd Amy Stokes was so buried in the crossway Beyond
sparrowes corner neare to the place wheare the owld cross
ded stand the sayd vij^th Day of September ano 1590
abowte the owere of viij or ix of the clocke at nyght she
was abowte three skore yeares owld.

This grisly account is of special interest. One who died
by suicide—a felo-de-se—was particularly abhorred as a person who had destroyed himself. In so doing he had, like Amy
Stokes, "fallen from God." The attitude of the Church in
Tudor times is clearly reflected in the law (4 George 4,
cap. 52) that was passed more than two centuries later to do
away with some of the unrelenting penalties invoked for

suicides. It is remarkable that this legal reform, incomplete as it was, did not take place until 1823. The law was entitled

> *An act to alter and amend the law relating to the interment of the remains of any person found Felo de se.*—Whereas it is expedient that the laws and usages relating to the interment of the remains of persons, against whom a finding of *felo de se* shall be had, should be altered and amended: be it therefore enacted by the king's most excellent majesty, by and with the advice and consent of the lords spiritual and temporal . . . that . . . it shall not be lawful for any coroner, or other officer having authority to hold inquests, to issue any warrant or other process directing the interment of the remains of persons, against whom a finding of *felo de se* shall be had, in any public highway; but that such coroner or other officer shall give directions for the private interment of the remains of such persons *felo de se,* without any stake being driven through the body of such person, in the churchyard or other burial ground of the parish. [Law 1847]

However, the 1823 law still required that the interment of the suicide

> be made within twenty-four hours of the finding of the inquisition, and . . . take place between the hours of nine and twelve at night.
>
> Provided nevertheless, that nothing herein contained shall authorize the performing of any of the rites of christian

burial on the interment of the remains of any such person as aforesaid; nor shall anything hereinbefore contained be taken to alter the laws or usages relating to the burial of such persons.

In other words, the 1823 law made it no longer legal for a coroner to direct that a suicide be buried in a public highway or that a stake be driven through the body, but the remains still had to be denied Christian burial and be interred between 9 P.M. and midnight. It is difficult to believe that such barbarous practices had in fact persisted until the nineteenth century, regardless of the law, but they certainly were observed in the case of Amy Stokes.

The basis for all this seems to go back very far. The early Teutonic tribes performed human sacrifices on altars that many times were built at crossroads. Often the victims were criminals; their remains were buried on the spot. From this grew the practice of public executions at crossroads and of the burial of the criminals and the equally abhorred suicides at the site. Tyburn, where the gallows stood in Shakespeare's day, lay outside London at the junction of what were then the Edgware, Oxford, and London Roads (Anon. 1937; MacCulloch 1912). Such a triple branching or fork constituted the ancient Latin *trivium,* the three ways.[30] Hecate, the mysterious goddess of darkness, terror, and witchcraft,

---

30. Hence our word *trivial.* Itinerant peddlers set up their displays at the point where a road forked. If there were executions and crowds came to watch, so much the better. *Trivial* was first applied to the cheap, unimportant items that the peddlers sold.

haunted graveyards and crossroads. As the deity of the *trivium*, she was sometimes represented as a triple-headed figure (Brown 1966). Down through the Middle Ages the fork of a road was a frightening place after night fell. Sometimes a cross was erected there, perhaps to counteract the malign spirits thought to haunt the spot and perhaps also to comfort the families of criminals and suicides whose bodies rested under the highway. Amy Stokes was buried "in the crossway Beyond sparrowes corner neare to the place wheare the owld cross ded stand."

The religious horror with which suicide was regarded is further revealed by the fact that its victims could not be laid in a churchyard, although this privilege, as we learn from the St. Botolph records, was not withheld in the case of murderers and other executed criminals.

The practice of driving a stake through a body—actually, through the heart—goes back to the vampire superstition (Anon. 1937; Atkinson 1898). The stake was believed to prevent the vampire from leaving his grave in order to seek victims. Extension of the stake's use to the bodies of suicides perhaps originated as a precaution to keep their ghosts from returning to haunt former companions (MacCulloch 1912, 1922).

Burial of suicides at night may well have been begun as a rite in honor of Hecate, goddess of darkness. Continuation of the practice, as required even by the 1823 law for interment of suicides, probably was in recognition of the practical advantage of deferring the burial until most people were off the streets and roads and night had fallen, the ceremony thereby arousing a minimum of public notice. Even when the Church gave its consent to the interment of suicides in holy ground, conservative parishioners could hardly have welcomed such graves in their churchyards.

About five years after the Amy Stokes tragedy, another death and burial much like hers occurred. The coroner's inquest, again called by Thomas Wilbraham, met on Friday morning, 28 November 1595, in St. Botolph's

> to Inquyre owt howe Elizabeth Wickham a widow being an Incontinent[31] person did come to her death, who had hanged her selfe upon a garden pale in her aperne stringe: her selfe sitting as it weare upon the ground The garden pales whereon she hanged her selfe did some tyme belong to one M[r] Dowlman, & is amongst the gardens neare hogg lane & in the precinct of howsdich It is said she lept [in] a noell [an hole] the day before in scommer aley being in hownsdich was taken out agayne at that tyme alyve This said Elizabeth Wickham was buried the said xxviij[th] day of November anno 1595 in the aley where she hanged her selfe according to her dezarts having a stake driven thorowgh her in Remembrance of her wicked [act?— partly illegible]. She was about some xxxvj yeares owld.

A notation in the margin adds, "Elizabeth Wickhan buried according to hir dezarts in an Alye being comon thorowgh-fare or highway."

31. Unchaste.

Here again is the specified treatment of the suicide—condemnation by the Church, burial in a highway, the stake. But no mention of what drove the widow to her pathetic death.

On 13 April 1598 Mistress Elizabeth Townsend, wife of John Townsend, citizen and fletcher of London and a member of St. Botolph's Parish, died in childbirth at the age of forty-four. She was being cared for by a woman whose name was not recorded. This nurse, who apparently stayed on in the Townsend home, took her own life some weeks later—she "was said to have hanged hir selfe in the said howse." The coroner's inquest met in the parish church on the afternoon of 25 May 1598, and "shee was buried the said nyght in hogg lane."

> Mary Play, a Maid of Eastsmithfield, who poysened hir selfe, in the house of hir Maister, Mr John Barbour, was by a License from my Lord Bishoppe of London buried in our new Church-yard without any buriall service.

Here, it would seem, there were extenuating circumstances that justified a special episcopal license, but even so there could be no rite of interment.

The last of the seven suicides was that of John Blackman, mentioned earlier (p. 31), who wounded himself in a delirium. It will be recalled that the coroner's inquest held that he was not responsible, and "order was apointed to have him laid in Christian Buriall."

The accidental and violent deaths described in this chapter

are summarized in tables 10 and 11. Half of all the deaths were accidents. Distribution of deaths by month was fairly even, with the exception of murders and executions. Eight of 32 murders occurred in May. Of 17 executions, five were carried out in July and eight in August, but this may have been because the assizes were held in the summer. Male deaths exceeded, usually by a wide margin, those of females in every category except suicide. Seven suicides in 52

Table 10. Accidental and Violent Deaths by Sex and Month of Occurrence, 1573–1624

	Drownings	Falls	Crushings, Blows	Manslaughter	Burns	Horses, Carts	Guns, Gunpowder	Asphyxiation	Murders	Executions	Suicides
Male	12	10	4	5	2	3	3	1	21	16	1
Female	8		1		2	1		1	11	1	6
Unknown	1		1								
Jan.	1			1	1	1			3		
Feb.	1	1		1	2				1		
Mar.		1							1		1
April		1		1					1	3	
May	4		1	1					8	1	1
June	3	1					2		1		
July	2	1	3	1		1		1	4	5	1
Aug.	3	2							3	8	1
Sept.	2	1	1			1			1		1
Oct.	2								2		1
Nov.		1			1	1	1		3		1
Dec.	3	1	1					1	4		

years (1573–1624) seems a very small number. In 1967 in England and Wales the annual suicide rate per 100,000 population was 12.1 for males and 8.8 for females (Anon. 1968).

The distribution of the 55 accidental deaths by age group is rough, since in a number of cases exact age at death was

Table 11. Accidents by Age Group, 1573–1624

	Drownings	Falls	Crushings, Blows	Manslaughter	Burns	Horses, Carts	Guns, Gunpowder	Asphyxiation	Total
2–6 months		1			1				2
7–11									
1 year									
2	1				1	1			3
3	2				1				3
4									
5–6	1								1
7–9	1								1
10–14	2		1	1		1			5
15–19	1	1						1	3
20–29	1	1	1	3			1		7
30–39	1		1				1		3
40–49				1					1
50–59									
60–69		1							1
Children	3	1	1		1	1			7
Adults	7	5	2			1	1	1	17
Unknown	1								1
Total	21	10	6	5	4	4	3	2	55

not recorded. In these cases I have categorized the victims as "Children" or "Adults." If individuals of known age through the ten- to fourteen-year-old group are added to the group labeled "Children," and if "Adults" are similarly combined with the older groups, it will be seen that drownings had about equal distribution (ten children, eleven adults). Seven of the eight deaths caused by burns or by carts and horses were those of children. Adults were the victims of most of the other accidents.

VII: Care of the Indigent Sick

The burden of care of the indigent, including the sick, fell heavily on the parishes of England in the sixteenth and seventeenth centuries. The obligation of each parish to meet the needs of the poor who lived within it had been established as a legal principle by 1388 (Gray 1963). During the Middle Ages the monasteries had done much to supply food, alms, shelter, and some medical care to the ill and poverty-stricken. The Church by no means met all the needs, and it had the funds to do much more, but at least it provided a form of organized charity that gave limited relief.

However, in the first part of the sixteenth century this mechanism collapsed, just when it began to be needed more than ever. Henry VIII had been quarreling with the Church.

His resentment of papal intervention in affairs of the realm led him to seek from Parliament a series of restrictive measures that strengthened his hand considerably; the Act of Supremacy, passed in 1534, established the dominant position of the Crown. Henry needed the wealth of the monasteries, and looked for an excuse to acquire it. When Cromwell sent out agents to inspect the religious houses and their activities, they brought back reports of laxity of discipline, neglect, and corruption. The reports were exaggerated, but they served Henry's purpose, and he dissolved the monastic orders. By seizing their lands and other wealth and distributing them to the nobility and landed gentry, he greatly weakened the power of the Church and at the same time increased his popularity with, and support from, the most influential segment of the population.

The collapse of the system of charity hitherto provided by the monasteries was disastrous. The British economy was in a bad way. Seizure of arable lands by the mechanism of enclosure was in effect depriving great numbers of peasants of their means of making a living. Rents rose sharply. The village workers lost their miserable homes. Hungry and desperate, the country folk swarmed to the cities to look for work and food. This only exacerbated urban unemployment, overcrowding, shortage of food, and poverty. In the last quarter of the sixteenth century the price of grain rose steadily as the supply diminished. The scarcity became particularly acute in 1594–98 due to successive crop failures caused by excessive rain and cold. Conditions sank almost to a famine level. There were bread riots in London in 1595.[1]

Parliament may not have been fully aware of the situation in rural areas, but it could not ignore the throngs of the poor and needy on the streets of London. Many of these people, whether by choice or necessity, had become vagabonds, beggars, or worse. Crime and disorder had been rampant throughout the century, and increasingly harsh and repressive measures had been devised by the authorities (Rowse 1951). A partial list of this legislation includes *An Act Concerning Egyptians*[2] and *An Act Concerning the Punishment of Beggars and Vagabonds* in 1530, a supplementary act in 1535, *An Act for the Punishment of Vagabonds, and for the Relief of the Poor and Impotent Persons* in 1547, and additional punitive laws in 1551 and 1555.[3]

But the problem continued. Parliament was still in large part seeking to deal with the results of poverty rather than with its causes. Whipping, the stocks, and branding stopped neither hunger and cold nor the crimes that they engendered in desperate men, women, and children. Elizabeth I inherited the evil from her predecessors and in turn sought to find a solution.[4] In 1562 Parliament passed a law (5 Eliz. 1, cap. 3)

1. Gibbons 1969; Jordan 1959; Lunt 1957.

2. Gypsies.

3. Nicholls reviews the acts in detail in *A History of the English Poor Law* (1854).

4. The following brief review is based on Anon. 1636; Gray 1963; Jordan 1959; Nicholls 1854; Ribton-Turner 1887; Strype 1754; and Webb 1927.

confirming much of the earlier legislation regarding the collection of alms for the indigent. Persons who refused to contribute were subject to fine and imprisonment. If a parish had more poor people than it could support, they were permitted to beg elsewhere, but only within limits specified by a license. Another act in the same year (5 Eliz. 1, cap. 4) was intended to force all able-bodied persons to work.

An order was issued by the City of London in 1569 for the Preventing of all idle Persons and begging People, whether Men, Women, or Children, or other masterless Vagrants ... to take them all up, and to dispose of them in some of the four Hospitals[5] in *London,* by the sixteen Beadles belonging to the same, who had their several Standings and Walks in every Ward. Those that were Vagabonds and sturdy Beggars, they were to carry to *Bridewell.* Those that were aged, impotent, sick, sore, lame, or blind, to *St. Bartholomew's* or *St. Thomas's* Hospital. And all Children under the Age of sixteen to *Christ's* Hospital. And this order was made at a Meeting of the Governours of all the Hospitals.

The order went on to direct that beadles be on duty at all the City gates, London Bridge, and specified wharfs to watch for and "apprehend the Vagabonds, Beggars, Children, and Masterlesse men and Women" (Strype 1754).

5. The term "hospital" at that time meant a refuge or shelter. Only St. Bartholomew's and St. Thomas's cared for the sick.

In 1572 an important statute (14 Eliz. 1, cap. 5), *An Act for the Punishment of Vagabonds and for Relief of the Poor and Impotent,* was enacted. It complained that the country was

> presently with rogues, vagabonds, and sturdy beggars exceedingly pestered, by means whereof daily happeneth horrible murders, thefts, and other great outrages, to the high displeasure of Almighty God, and to the great annoyance of the common weal.

The act directed that beggars aged fifteen or over were to be arrested: if found guilty they were to be "grievously whipped, and burnt through the gristle of the right ear with a hot iron of the compass of an inch about" unless "some honest person will of his charity take such offender into his service for one whole year next following." For a second offense the prisoner would be punished as a felon. The penalty for the third offense was "death, and loss of lands and goods, as a felon, without allowance of benefit of clergy or sanctuary." The definition of "rogues, vagabonds, and sturdy beggars" was extremely broad, including not only able-bodied persons who were not employed but palmists, fortune tellers, fencers, players, jugglers, tinkers, petty chapmen, counterfeit "Scollers of the Universityes of Oxford or Cambridge y^t goe about begginge," and many others. The act then went on to make some provision for the aged and impotent poor, directing that places should be found for them to settle and that local inhabitants should be taxed to provide the funds. If one community could not supply enough money, others would be forced to help.

According to Stow, this legislation was quite effective. He reports:

> By the care of *Fleetwood* the Recorder[6] and the other Magistrates, in the Year 1575, there were few or no Rogues and Thieves in the Gaol; for the Lord-keeper *Bacon,* in the Month of *August,* sitting in the *Star-Chamber,* and, according to the Order, calling for the Book of Misbehaviours of masterless Rogues, Fencers, and such-like, there was none to present for *London;* though for *Surry* there were five or six Strumpets, that had lately been punished at the Assizes at *Croyden:* and *Westminster,* the Dutchy, [that is, the Places about *St. Clement's* and the *Savoy*][7] *St. Giles, High-Holborn,* St. *John's-street* and Islington, great Harbours of such misdemeaned Persons, were never so well or quiet. For Rogue nor masterless Man dared not once to appear in those Parts; into such good Order had the Care of the Magistrate at this Time brought the City and Suburbs. [Strype 1754]

But in spite of Stow's optimism, vagrancy and related problems continued, and more laws were forthcoming. An act *For some better Explanation, and for some needful Addition to the Statute concerning the Punishment of Vagabonds and Relief of the Poor* (18 Eliz. 1, cap. 3) in 1575 made

6. A chief magistrate.
7. This interpolation is by Strype, the editor of Stow's *Survey.*

special provision for the support of illegitimate children, the parents being held responsible. Arrangements were outlined for the employment of young people, and houses of correction were set up for vagabonds. Adult rogues upon reaching these institutions were to be stripped to the waist and given twelve strokes of the whip; young offenders got six. The whip "shal be made with twoe cordes withowte knotts." The severity of these and other punishments was somewhat reduced in 1593 (35 Eliz. 1, cap. 7).

A new law in 1597 (39 Eliz. 1, cap. 4) had little that was original regarding rogues and vagabonds. Once again the earlier laws were repealed, and once again the new law enumerated the offenders:

All persons calling themselves Schollars, going about begging, all Sea faring men pretending losses of their ships or goods on the Sea . . . all idle persons . . . either begging or using any subtile craft, or unlawfull games and playes, or faining themselves to have knowledge in Physiognomie, Palmestry, or other like crafty Science, or pretending that they can tell Destinies, fortunes, or such other like fantasticall imaginations: All persons that be, or utter themselves to be Proctors, Procurers, Patent-gatherers, or Collectors for Gaoles, prisons or Hospitals: All fencers, Bearewardes,[8] Common Players of Interludes, and Minstrels, wandering abroad (other then Players of Interludes belonging to any Baron of this Realme, or any other hon-

8. Persons who kept bears.

ourable personage of greater degree, to bee authorized to play under the hand and Seale of Armes of such Baron or personage), all Juglers, Tinkers, Pedlars, and pety Chapmen wandering abroad, all wandering persons and common Labourers, being persons able in body, using loytering, and refusing to worke for such reasonable wages . . . All persons delivered out of Gaoles that begge for their fees, or otherwise do travaile begging: All such persons as shall wander abroad begging, pretending losses by fire, or otherwise: And all such persons not being felons, wandering and pretending themselves to bee Egyptians . . . shall be taken, adivdged [adjudged], and deemed Rogues, Vagabonds, and sturdy beggers.

Offenders were to be

stripped naked from the middle upwards, and shall bee openly whipped untill his or her body be bloody; and shall be forthwith sent from parish to parish by the Officers of every the same, the next straight way to the parish where he was borne.

If the prisoner's parish were not known, he was to be returned to the last parish where he had lived before his present offense, after having been passed along from one parish to the next.[9] A special exception was made for mariners who

9. Jordan (1959) points out the importance of such regulations, which represent an effort "towards the sealing off of poverty within the parish in which the poor man was resident." One such unfortu-

had been shipwrecked and could prove it; they could be licensed to collect alms.

The provisions of the law covered much other ground, but these excerpts make clear its nature. It was supplemented in the same year by 39 Eliz. 1, cap. 17, which was concerned specifically with the control of pretended soldiers and sailors "abusing the title of that honourable profession to countenance their wicked behaviour." They were alleged to be wandering about in armed bands

> to the great terror and astonishment of her Majesty's true subjects. And many heinous outrages, robberies, and horrible murders are daily committed by these dissolute persons.

This law was replaced in 1601 by 43 Eliz. 1, cap. 3, a more charitable act that provided for the relief of genuine soldiers and sailors who were in distress.

While Parliament was struggling with control of the vagabonds, it was also making intermittent efforts to help the needy.[10] The first law for this purpose in Elizabeth's time

---

nate could not finish the hard journey back to his birthplace but ended his life in St. Botolph's Parish.

William Jones a vagrant who was said to be borne at Avelie in Essex he did lye sick in the cadge being in the libertie of East-smithfield where he dyed and was buried the xiij[th] day of November Anno 1597. yeares xviij he was no parishioner with us he was lame & his toes weare rotted off.

10. My account of the poor laws is drawn from Anon. 1937; Gray 1936; Jordan 1959; Lunt 1957; Nicholls 1854; Trotter 1919; and Webb 1927.

was passed in 1562 (5 Eliz. 1, cap. 3). It directed that if after persuasion by the curate, the churchwardens, and finally by the bishop alms were not forthcoming from a householder who was asked to contribute, the offender could be brought into court. There the justice of the peace was to urge once again that a donation be made; if the householder were still obstinate, he could be sent to prison until he offered what the court felt was a reasonable sum. Thus for the first time was the English public subjected to compulsory assessment to provide relief for the poor. The act was supplemented by another in the same year, 5 Eliz. 1, cap. 4, aimed at forcing all able-bodied persons to accept employment, thereby attempting to eliminate begging and dependency. Ten years later *An Act for the Punishment of Vagabonds, and for Relief of the Poor and Impotent* (14 Eliz. 1, cap. 5), previously referred to, provided for the establishment of institutions where aged poor people could live. Justices of the peace were to tax the population for the necessary funds, to arrange for their distribution, and to appoint overseers of the poor. The overseers were to handle the actual collection and disbursement of the money. This legislation in effect, provided the first all-embracing poor law. Unfortunately, we do not know much about how successful it was in operation. (There is a note in the St. Botolph record that on 19 February 1586 one John Taylor "was Excominicated for not paienge serten monye to the poore.")

Legislation intended to secure assistance for the indigent was clarified and greatly strengthened by *An Act for the Re-*

lief of the Poor (39 Eliz. 1, cap. 3), passed by Parliament in 1597. This important law, based on the experience of the century then about to end, faced up honestly to the problem of poverty. It provided that in every parish the churchwardens, together with four other substantial parishioners, should function as overseers of the poor. They were to find work for unemployed and indigent persons, including neglected children; to levy taxes, weekly or otherwise, on "every inhabitant, and every occupier of lands in the said parish"; to find materials—wool, hemp, flax, thread, and so on—"to set the poor on work"; and to provide relief for the "lame, impotent, old, blind, and such other among them being not able to work." The overseers could bind poor boys and girls as apprentices. Funds were also to be raised for assistance to prisoners and to the inhabitants of almshouses in the county.

This very significant legislation laid responsibility squarely on the parish, which was expected to look after not only its own but also other indigent persons coming within its boundaries. If any parish were unable to raise sufficient funds, the justices of the peace could levy rates on adjacent parishes for help. The mechanism was set up by the national government, but responsibility for operation of the plan was clearly established at the level of the parish, which was likewise held responsible for effective relief of the poor and for elimination of mendicancy. The Poor Law Act underwent only minor changes for more than two hundred years.

In 1601 Parliament passed a supplementary law (43 Eliz. 1, cap. 2) that confirmed and modified earlier legislation. The responsibility of parents for the support of their children was extended to the grandparents if the father and mother were unable to provide adequately. The able-bodied poor who refused to work were to be punished. Those few persons permitted to beg were restricted to specified areas. Overseers of the poor who neglected their duties were to be fined.

Indigent people who were in addition sick and helpless of course presented special problems. Until the early part of the sixteenth century, it will be remembered, responsibility for such unfortunate persons had been taken mostly by the clergy, and the hospitals were usually operated by monastic orders.[11] These hospitals of course were quite unlike our modern ones, the institution in Tudor times functioning more as an almshouse and a shelter for the hopelessly ill and aged. During the reign of Henry VIII London's hospitals were fairly numerous. St. Thomas's Hospital was the infirmary of the Priory of St. Mary Overy in Southwark. The Priory and Hospital of St. Bartholomew were in Smithfield. Near the Tower was St. Katherine's Hospital. The former Savoy Palace housed a hospital founded by Henry VII. There were at least two Hospitals of St. Mary, one of which had originally been the Priory of the Monastery of St. Mary of

11. The following account of London's hospitals is based on Clark-Kennedy 1962; Dainton 1961; Garrison 1929; Graves 1947; McCurrich 1929; McInnes 1963; Mettler and Mettler 1947; Rowse 1951; and Whitteredge and Stokes 1961.

Bethlehem. It was taken by the Crown in 1375, began to house lunatics in 1403, and ultimately became an institution for the insane.[12] The Bridewell,[13] a house of correction for beggars and prostitutes, was originally a palace built by Henry VIII. It stood near Blackfriars' Bridge. Christ's Hospital was an orphanage.[14]

Dissolution of the monasteries under the Act of Supremacy forced all of London's hospitals to shut their doors. Henry VIII had promised to provide for the poor and sick, and his earlier legislation for their relief indicates that he may have intended to do so, but nothing happened. St. Bartholomew's closed in October 1539 and St. Thomas's in January 1540. St. Katherine's by the Tower, which had endowment for the support of thirteen aged persons, was given to a friend of the King as a political reward. Buildings were shut up or converted to other purposes, trained staffs were dispersed, and the sick and hungry were left to their misery.

The citizens of London, appalled by this development, joined with the Lord Mayor in requesting Henry to reopen the Hospitals of St. Thomas, St. Bartholomew, and St. Mary

12. Our term *bedlam* is a variant of Bethlehem or Bethlem.

13. The name came from the nearby well of St. Bridget or St. Bride.

14. It began as a part of the Grey Friars' Monastery in Newgate Street, and was chartered by Edward VI in 1553 as a charitable home for children without parents. Ultimately Christ's Hospital became a famous public school. Its pupils, once known as Blue Coat Boys because of their long blue woolen gowns, included Charles Lamb, Leigh Hunt, and Samuel Taylor Coleridge.

Cripplegate, but for several years he failed to act. Finally, in 1546 St. Bartholomew's was refounded, although with a very small staff. The next year Henry established an annual endowment of £1,000 for refurbishing the hospital. St. Mary's of Bethlehem was given by the King to the Corporation of the City of London in 1546 as a hospital "for distracted people." Just before Henry died in 1547 he made a further agreement with the City whereby it could use for hospital construction and maintenance the income from a large amount of Church property acquired by the City. This arrangement provided for the development and support of St. Bartholomew's, Bridewell, Christ Hospital, and Bethlehem. In 1553 Edward VI added St. Thomas's to the list. St. Thomas's endowment was supplemented by the transfer to it of the estates of the old Savoy Hospital, which had never really reopened. Actually, the income from these estates was supposed to be shared with Christ Hospital and the Bridewell but because these two hospitals already had endowment, St. Thomas's received the full income. This was fortunate, for the Hospital was crowded in spite of the fact that after its repair, authorized in 1551, it had reopened with 260 beds. Henry VIII and Edward VI received credit as the founders of the "Royal Hospitals," although reestablishment of these institutions was much more the result of the energy and generosity of the City and its citizens. However, aside from Bedlam, whose benefits were dubious, London's only two hospitals providing for the ill were St. Thomas's and St. Bartholomew's.

It is a remarkable fact that, despite the impressive growth of London's population in the next two centuries, these two continued until 1720 to offer the only hospital care for the sick.

Keeping in mind this background of slowly developing measures to control vagabondage, poverty, helplessness, and illness, we can turn once more to the Parish of St. Botolph without Aldgate and consider the impact on it of these urgent social problems. The records provide rich information which, though fragmentary, can be assembled into a reasonably clear picture.

One ready means for the communication of the government with the people was a proclamation to be read in all the churches. This was the method used by William Seabright, Lord Mayor of London, in December 1594. In each ward a "precept" was directed to the alderman for transmittal to the parish. Thus at St. Botolph's on the eighth of that month

> Mr Joseph Cardwell who ded suplie the place of our minister for the morning prayer ... ded read in our parishe churche a precept derected from the Lord Maio^r unto the Alderman of this the ward of Portsoken conteyning as Followet viz.

> Whereas dyvers poore people being Aged Lame and Impotent not able to live of them selves w^thout reliefe from others do wander abroad to begg in all parts of the Cittie

which owght to be relieved in the parishes where they
weare born or dwelt by the space of three yeares last past,
according to the lawes and statute of this Realme for the
avoyding whereof these shalbe in her M^a ties name straight-
ly[15] to chardge and comand you that p^re sently upon the
sight hereof ye call before yo^ur deputie, the beadle, all the
most hable [able] suffitient[16] inhabitants and every parson
vicar minister churchwarden of everie such severall parish
within your ward and take present[17] order that a vewe and
survey be made of all the poore w^t hin the same which use
to begg abroad, and by the advyce of the said inhabitants
to take order that no maner of suche poore be suffered
from henceforth to begg in any part of the cittie but [in-
stead be] relieved at home w^t hin the parishes where they
were borne or lastly dwelt by the said space of three yeares
according to the statute and that if upon the said vewe it
shall apeare that there are more suche poore people in
everie parishe w^t hin your ward then [than] such parishe
shalbe of them seves [selves] hable to relieve, then you
make present certifficat to me in writing of the name surname and nomber of the saide poore to the end such further
order may be taken therein for the reliefe and stayeing[18]
them at home from begging abroad as shalbe needfull and

15. Strictly.
16. Competent.
17. Immediate.
18. Keeping.

by the lawe is requyred. these shalbe also to requyer [and] comand by all best wayes and meanes yo^u can to perswad the parson & minister of everie such severall parishe from tyme to tyme as shalbe needfull to exhorte all the inhabitants of everie suche parishe upon the sondayes and holly [holy] dayes in time of devyne service to yeld there charitable benevolence towarde the succor and reliefe of such poore people whereof se you fayle not at your perill.

Cosby place my house this vijth of December 1594

Sibright

Here was the local application of statutes we have already considered at the national level—statutes dealing with the problem of the beggars, the need for a survey of their numbers, the obligation of the parishes where the beggars were born or lived in the last three years, the provision of outside help if necessary, and finally, the requirement that the parish be exhorted to give alms.

There is another memorandum (23 January 1596) that Master Paul Bushey, the curate, read a precept from the Lord Mayor during morning service "For further order to be taken in the saide warde [of Portsoken] for the better relieving of the poore."

Most of the money to help the needy had to be raised the hard way, but there was a fascinating exception on 8 August 1592, when

an owld Anttient cittizen being a tall man with a long

black gray barde [beard] being acompanied with a young man being a high dutchman who would not be knowne unto me being the parishe clarke ded put into our poore box the some of twentie shillings . . . and would not be knowne whose gifte it was but willed that it should be by the churchwardens distributed to the poore of the parishe.

And not another word about the kind of windfall that every hard-pressed congregation must dream about—and pray for.

At least one guild contributed to charity. There are two references (14 December 1607; 12 January 1615) to individuals identified as "the Marchantaylors Almeswomen." One of these ladies was said to be one hundred years old.

St. Botolph's Parish also received funds annually from Christ's Hospital. Probably this was the parish's share of income from rents or endowment. We read that on 6 August 1589 the accounts for the past thirteen months of John Bolderstone and James Stone, collectors for the poor, were reviewed by the minister, churchwardens, and others. During this period

they have gathered . . . the some of sixtiene pounds three shillings and fower pence and there was receyved from Chryste hospitall the sayd thertiene monethes at x^s ix^d the monethe the whiche is vi^{lb} xix^s ix^d, all of which receipts do amount to the some of twentie and thre pounds three shillings and a penye. this accompt was awdited the first days of the moneth of September ano 1589.

The auditors also found that the collectors had paid out to the poor pensioners and to the hospital a total of £23 3s. 8d., or 7d. more than had been received. We must assume that payments to the hospital were for care provided there for indigent parish youngsters.

There was similar auditing of the accounts on 9 September 1590 and on 10 September 1595. On the latter occasion it was learned that during the past thirteen months the collectors for the poor had taken in £15 17s. 3d. and had received £6 19s. 9d. from Christ's Hospital. Payments "by the said collectors unto the poore pentioners of this our said parish and to the hospitall" totalled £23 3s. 8d., or 6s. 8d. more than received.

Foundlings,[19] neglected children, and orphans presented the parish with problems.

Marie a chylde that was founde in the streete beyond the widowe carltons Dore in the high waye neare a Dunghill whose father and mother was not knowne beinge nurssed by henrie Mawkenews wyfe in Barnarde Alye being Beyond mineries [Minories] was buried the xv^th Daye of marche ano 1588 beinge a crisom and beinge jawefallen.

19. If the parents of an abandoned baby were not known, the parish supplied a last name. Thus we read of "John foundelinge an infant" (27 January 1584)—"foundling" was a common designation —of "Lancaster Stall, a Bastard so named because it was laid uppon the stall of one Miles Lancaster, a Cooke in the high street" (31 January 1601), and of "Edward Portsoken a Child left in the ward of portsoken and kept by ye Inhabitants there" (13 March 1622).

A Chrisome borne in Jacobe well yeard, daughter to a strumpet, who ranne a way, left yt. [22 March 1609]

The parish was obliged to care for such infants, but it was careful not to acquire possible future responsibility when, for example, it permitted baptism of the child of known non-parishioners.

Robert Keyo the sonn of Jhon Keyo was cristened the xxij daye of December in ano 1583 beinge no parishioners chyld the mother of this chylde was brought a bed in ye house of anthonye bell a carpender dwellinge in ye high streate and ye father of this chylde is bownde to ye church-wardens of this parish in a bond of Ten pounds to dis-chardge the parish of the chyld the wch bond is in ye hande of richard casye nowe beinge ye aldermans Deputie of this ower warde of portsoken extra algate.

Thus, if for any reason the child should some day become a public charge, St. Botolph's Parish could not be held liable without forfeiture of the bond to the parish. There were numerous similar cases, usually involving a baby born within the parish to a father and mother who were not parishioners. Robert Cramphorne, christened 24 March 1583 in Hounds-ditch, had such parents.

The parishe hath bonde to save them [the parish] harme-les[20] from beinge charged any time or waye about this chylde. the Bond M^r deputie has.

20. Free of liability.

Jhon Mulford . . . was cristned the xxix[th] daye of June in
ano 1584 . . . And M[r] Deputie Did take order with y[e]
frend of this chylde, for that it sholod [should] not be
chargable to y[e] parish for that it is no parishioners chyld.

Jhon Ethill the sonne of Thomas Ethill a husband man . . .
and bonde being made to the aldermans deputie for the
discharge of the parish the sayd chyld was cristned the vth
day of September ano 1589.

Suzana Ruffer the dawghter of Peter Ruffer a marchannt
strang[r] whose wyfe named Jereene Ruffer was browght a
bed in the howse of lieven Allette a dutch midwyfe dwelling in the Dewkes place being within algate wheare the
sayd chyld was borne and bonde being made by Jhon De
grave a shoomaker dwelling in whyt chapell parish peter
Snedins also a shoomaker dwelling in the Dewkes place
unto Charles Russell and Jhon Woodrose churchwardens
of this parishe for the savinge of the parish from being
chardged with the said chyld. the said chyld was christned
the iiij[th] Day of September ano 1591 and the said Bond
is in the hands of M[r] Russell.

Mary Matthews, born to parents from Gloucestershire, was
christened 30 August 1612 in St. Botolph's Church. "There
were Suertyes taken to discharge the Parish of y[e] said Child."

Sara Hutton the Reputed Daughter of one Thomas Hutton,
and Francis his reputed wife, who was Delivered of Child

in the house of Edward Clark Turner in houndsditch, the
said Child was Christened the fifteenth day of Februarie
Anno Dni 1620.

Thus wee were informed, but God knoweth, whether it
be true or not. Sureties were taken to discharg ye parish.

Although Christ's Hospital existed for the purpose of
caring for homeless children, I found mention of only one
instance in which the Parish of St. Botolph approached it for
help. There is a notation that at a vestry meeting

a request was made to the mastere of Christes hospitall to
take into there . . . Hester Plomton the daughter of
Isabell Plomton Beinge of the age of three yeares.

On the other hand, the records carry dozens of entries regarding care given to children in foster homes. These homes
were not necessarily within the parish.

Memerandum that charles Russell being Renteror For
the poore Lande[21] ded paye unto Barnard Fishe of hatfield
Brodorke [Broad Oak?] beinge nors [nurse] y^t doth norse
Jhon Williams a chylde kept at the charges of the parishe
the third day of October in ano 1587 and was for xxvii
weekes Dewe [due] unto hem the xxx daye of September
Last past at viij^d the weeke the some of xxiij^d and more he
payde unto hem the same tyme to bye thinges necesarie

21. Rent collector for properties whose income went to the poor.

for the sayde childe the some of xi^s viiij^d. So that he payde him in all at this time the some of xxiiij^s viij^d.[22]

The next day it was noted that another child, George Tydy,

left upon the parishes hands to be kepte was put to Norse to one Barnard fishe a joyner dwellinge at Hatfield brodock in Essex.

Fish received a down payment of 3d. for the support of the Tydy child, and in addition 2d. was given to one Elizabeth Kempton for delivering the boy to Fish. Thereafter there were intermittent payments totaling 22s. in (calendar) 1587, 59s. 4d. in 1588, 96s. 8d. in 1589, 112s. 10d. in 1590, 65s. 4d. in 1591, 47s. in 1592, 46s. in 1593, and 62s. through 18 December 1594. The charges were for "nourishing," i.e., food and board, and for "aparell" and "other things neccesarie." An itemized list of the latter, presented to the parish 1 October 1590, reads:

Item for a greene cote for george tydie	iij^s	iiij^d
Item for a jourkin[23] and a payer of gaskins[24] for Jhon Williams	v^s	iiij^d
Item for a hat for george tydye		vj^d
Item for ij sherts	ij^s	iiij^d
Item for ij payer of shoose		xvj^d

22. At 8d. the week for 27 weeks Barnard Fish would have been due 18s. Presumably he had received part of this amount earlier.

23. A jerkin, a close fitting jacket or waistcoat.

24. Gaiters.

Item for ij payer of hose		x^d
Item for xiiij weekes of schoolling of		
Jhon Williams at iij^d the weeke	iij^s	vj^d
Item for chardgis in bringing the sayd		
children up to London that the par-		
ishe myght see the children		v^d
Some	xvij^s	vij^d

It is somewhat reassuring to learn from the last item that the parish officials had the two boys taken to London for inspection, apparently the first such occasion since January 1587. On 18 December 1594 Barnard Fish

> was willed to bring the elder chyld named Jhon Williams home to the masters of this parishe at christmas next for that the masters weare to put the said chyld to service.[25]

There was a final payment of 10s. on 22 December for John's care, and we hear no more about him. Payments for George Tydy's board and lodging continued for a while, 13s. 8d. on 28 December 1594, 31s. in 1595, 44s. 4d. in 1596, and 8s. 8d. in 1597.

Susan Olliver, "A poore fatherles chyld," was also supported by the parish. Payments for her food and shelter were made to the wife of John Mullett, who lived in the Parish of St. Magdalen Bermondsey, south of the Thames. For her maintenance St. Botolph's Church spent 10s. in 1588, 26s.

25. That is, to have him begin an apprenticeship.

8d. in 1589, 20s. in 1590, 14s. 8d. in 1591, and 3s. in 1592. Elizabeth Wolfe received for the support and clothing of William Sturgion, "a chyld kept by the parish," 32s. 6d. in 1594, 34s. in 1595, and 6s. in 1596. Payments are also recorded for the care of three other girls.

Burial records tell us of a number of additional poor children for whom the parish made arrangements. Robert Phillips was looked after in a widow's home,

> beinge turned upon the parishe by the mayor for that the father was in service in Fraunce because it [the child] was borne in this parishe. [21 December 1589]

A male infant, said to be a sailor's son, was born 9 May 1596 to

> a single woman who was delivered of the said chyld in the streete before the dore of the house of Thomas harrydance[26] being in the way as we go toward the mynories.... [The mother] taking the said chyld into her lap was conducted by dyvers women unto the house of Robert Acton a tipler as then dwelling at the signe of the Ellyfant being in the libertie of Eastsmithfield [with] whome she did lately dwell and the said Robert Acton at the apoyntment of the constables of the said libertie Asigned her with her chyld [to] lye at the house of William Cooke a smithe dwelling in pond alley.

26. Clerk of the parish at the time.

Here we see clearly the operation of the parish mechanism for arranging care for a youngster. However, the continuation of such care was uncertain, and neglect and lack of supervision could make life dreadful, while it lasted, for a foster child.

> Paludia Foord a Base-borne Child nursed in the house of Thomas Overlin a Tyncker of Rosemarie lane (where it was base-lie used, and Starved).

The child was buried 31 January 1621.

> Marie Sedway the Reputed Daughter of one John Sedway a Shoemaker of Chauncerie Lane (as wee were informed) y^t was Nursed in the house of one Edith Jones a poore widow of east smithfeild, where it died. . . . There are verie few Children prosper Long in our Parish, that are Nursed in such Places. [31 October 1623]

Another little girl, "Daughter to one John Carey that serveth the Lord Deputie of Ireland," did not survive her stay in a collier's home; "hee that loveth his dogg would not put it in such a place to be brought upp" (6 April 1624).

Some church members were sympathetic toward the children's plight, and some were not. Eight vestrymen met on 12 August 1597; one of them blocked an attempt at good works.

> Memorandum that dyvers vestrie men of the upper end of the parish of St Buttolphes without Aldgate London

> called the ward of Portsoken in tender regard of the
> greate nomber of poore children that was fallen upon there
> hands to be relieved and having smale store of money
> whereby to defray the chardge for to continew the re-
> lieveing of them did assemble togither . . . in the after-
> noone about the ower of two of the clock with determyna-
> tion to have seassed [assessed] them selves towards the
> said good godly and charytable worke of relieving of
> Children at which tyme by the meanes of the untowardnes
> of Mr Richard Casye being one of the vestrie men then
> assembled, There was nothing done at the said meeting.

Those familiar, hollow words! Fortunately there were some
church members who did not give up easily. Eight days later,
on a Saturday afternoon,

> Mr Nycholas and dyvers of the Inhabitants dwelling within
> the ward of Portsoken without Aldgate did assemble them
> selves togither in the parish church . . . [and] did set downe
> and conclud upon a certain seasement for the keeping of
> the xj children wch were to be kept by the said ward.

The support of eleven children must have been a difficult
burden for a church also obliged to provide alms repeatedly
for the adult poor, particularly when, as we know, the parish
itself was by no means well-to-do. Judging from the numerous entries over the years recording burials of infants and
children supported by St. Botolph's Church, we can see that
it probably was not unusual for the parish to be faced with
the care of a dozen youngsters at one time.

And providing for homeless children was only the beginning of the parish's charitable responsibilities. There was a steady stream of needy adults for whom funds had to be found. We do not know the extent of the parish's generosity in the period from 1558 until 1583, for the record is silent regarding donations during those years. Collectors for the poor must have been appointed before 1591, for on 27 June of that year it is noted that a precept from the Lord Mayor of London was read out in church ordering that new collectors were to be chosen and were to serve for one year. A vestry meeting was duly held the same day after morning prayer, and Daniel Peterson, citizen and merchant tailor, and Cuthbert Donn, citizen and farrier, were named. The election of new collectors is noted again on 23 June 1594; the procedure very likely was an annual formality. It is also recorded that four overseers for the poor, one for each precinct in the Ward of Portsoken, were appointed from the church membership on 25 April 1617.

Whether by design or chance, an interesting mechanism for relief of the destitute developed under the Poor Laws. This was the licensed soliciting of funds by impoverished individuals. It was not professional begging in the usual sense, for the suppliant could present both a legitimate appeal for help he clearly needed and deserved and an official sanction of his request. Let us see how this operated.

Memerandum that a collexion was gathered in ower parishe churche by one Thomas Butler dwellinge in cowl-chester who gathered the same by vertewe of a lycence granted him from ye Bishop of London For ye cittie of London midlesex and essex the wch Lycense so granted hem was Dated the first daye of June in ano 1583, and the sayde Thomas was by the sayde Lycence admitted to coleckt and gather ye good wille of the well disposed people in ye sayde cittie and sheares [shires, counties] above named the space of one whole yeare after ye date of the sayde Lysence and the Fore sayde Thomas ded collect and gather this viijth daye of Febrewarye in ower parishe churche in ano 1583 the some of ij s iij d and the same was ingrosed upon his Lysence bearinge Date ye Daye and yeare above sayde.

Thomas Butler's licensed solicitation is the earliest noted in the parish records. The clerk failed to give the reason for Butler's privation but thereafter the alms seeker's circumstances were almost always made clear.

Memerandum that a collection was gathered in ow^{er} parishe church the xxvijth Day of June anno 1591 by vertue of a lysence from her ma^{tis} high courte of the Admiraltie dated the vijth Day of march 1590 being grannted for the cittie of London and the suburbs of the same and the Borowgh of Southworke for one whole yeare after the date thereof and was for one Stephen Flint of London Dyer having served her Matie in the Lowe contries the space of seven yeares under Generall Norris was in the same service maymed and lost one of his hands and sence hath sustayned greate losse and hindrance by casualtie of fyer and thereby is falen into utter decay and povertie and not able to sustayne his poore wyfe and chyldren in consideration wheare of there was gathered for him at this instant tyme the some of three shillings and fower pence the wch money being ingrosed upon one of his briefs was delivered hem the therd Day of July 1591 by the parishe clarke.

Note that each license was officially issued for use during a specified period and that the alms received were inscribed on the license as well as in the parish record. Thus each parish visited could determine what had already been given. The method strikes one as being quite efficient. The needy individual could present his own case as eloquently as he knew how, speaking directly to his prospective benefactors. The state did not have to collect contributions itself; such a practice would have produced major administrative problems. The parish received some protection in that the alms seeker could not simply pocket each donation as it was received. Instead, the whole sum was collected, officially recorded, and only then turned over to the impoverished man. (Almost no requests from women are noted.)

A review of twenty-five entries regarding alms collected for needy persons shows that most licenses were good for one year, although occasionally they were also given for two months, six months, or two years. The license, also referred to as a passport or letters patent, might be issued by the Queen, the Privy Council, the Admiralty, the Bishop of London, the Lord Mayor of London, or a justice of the peace. The geographic area in which the license could be used, as noted by the clerk, might be London alone or might include Middlesex and sometimes Essex. At times the area was identified by the quaint phrase, "an alms roam," that is, the district in which the needy person was permitted to roam about seeking alms. In the case of an individual who must have been something of a national hero (see below), the license was for all of England. Amounts collected varied from a shilling up to as much as £3. 4s. 6d. when a ransom had to be raised (see below). In no instance was the recipient of alms a resident of St. Botolph's Parish; the parish took care of its own by other methods.

Notations in the parish records about the collection of alms are very numerous. The reasons why help was needed comprise a catalogue of personal disasters. Sometimes a man had been reduced to poverty by fire or shipwreck.

A collexion was gathered in yᵉ parishe church . . . By vertue of yᵉ Queens Maᵗⁱᵉ Brode seale being granted of Jhon Royon of yᵉ parishe of Allsaynts Barkinge who by yᵉ Loss of Dyvers shipps & other goods upon yᵉ north coste of England was greatlye Impoverished in consideration whereof this foresayd Brodsealle was granted hem bearinge Date yᵉ xiijᵗʰ Daye of September [1583] . . . and he was

Lycensed therbye to aske ye good wils of ye well disposed people w^t in this cittie of London for ye space of one whole yeare after ye date thereof.

Seven shillings were raised for him by the parish on 12 April 1584,

the wch sayd some beinge ingrossed upon the Letter patten was Delivered the same Daye and tyme unto his Deputie.

A collexion for one Laurence Sered who had grete Losse by fyer. [11 October 1584]

Memerandum that a collexion was gathered thorowgh owt the whole parish by Jhon Cowsell and Humphrie Rowland beinge churchwardens and was to relieve one Grigorie Pormorte of the cittie or towne of kingstone upon Hull who havinge lost nyne ships w^t his goods therein amount-inge to the some of manye thowsand pownds the Last whereof beinge a goodlie newe ship was sodenlye con-sumed by fyer in hull harbor to the grete astonishment of the whole towne of hull and the utter undoing of the sayde grigorie, his wyfe and children this sayde colexion was gathered for him By vertue of the Queenes ma^tie Letters pattens beinge grannted hem for one whole yeare.

The parish collected 33s. 4d on 12 January 1586 and

the wch monye beinge Ingrosed upon the Backe syd of the coppie of his Letters patens the sayde monye was Delivered

unto one Jhon Collins beinge his Deputie. . . . A Lysence
was puplished from the Lord Mayor for a collection to be
gathered about the ward for Mrs Haman, Thomas Martin
and Jhon Teay Cittizens of London hindred by fyer. [7 December 1589]

One wonders what happened to impoverished persons
when their licenses expired. No doubt by then some of them
had managed to regain their footing. Others may have fallen
anew into poverty. I did find records indicating that one individual held two different, successive licenses. It will be
recalled that Thomas Butler of Colchester had sought alms
successfully on 8 February 1583 and that the amount was en-
grossed on his license. On 14 September 1589, who should
turn up but Thomas Butler of Colchester, complete with a
license granted by the Bishop of London and good for one
year from 8 December 1588. This time the clerk gives more
information. Butler had

sustayned greate Loss of goods and [been] maymed of his
bodye by sodayne Fyer hapninge by makinge of gonpowder
for her ma^ties service to the utter undoing of him his wyfe
and children and therefore was granted unto him the re-
vertion of an almes roome in her hygnes [Highness]
cathedrall church of chryst in the universitie of oxford
when it shall happen to be voyd and beinge kept from the
same by the neames of former graunts he now by the sayd
lysence graunted to gather for his better reliefe the good

wills of the well disposed people inhabitinge w^{t}hin the countie of Essex and midlesex for one whole yeare.

This time 3s. 8d were collected for Butler. He seems to have been treated relatively well over the years; there is reference to "former graunts" as well as to the alms room that awaited him as soon as it became vacant. Perhaps he received special consideration because of his hazardous former occupation.

On Sunday, 22 February 1617, there was a "Collection upon the Kings Maiesties Letter Pattents" for

one Richard Hanwell of Bugbie in North-hampton shire, whose house and goods were Consumed by Casualtie of fire, and there was gathered for him the somme of Eighteen shillings, which was paid the same day to Joane his wife.

Again, on 16 January 1619:

There was collected in our parish Church for one John
Coston & others for losse by fire   vj^s viij^d
For one Jeremie Lascar a Grecian & I doubt a
Counterfairt [counterfeit] fellow.   vj^s iiij^d

The clerk's suspicion that the "Grecian" was an impostor may have been well founded.

A request for funds to ransom captives of the Turks or "infidels" was not rare. Probably most of the victims were

English sailors. Other mariners in need were those who had lost everything when their ships were attacked by pirates.

A collexion for one Mathew Roe of Dunster who had greate Losse at sea by pyrats. [9 July 1587]

A collection for Thomas Morgan who hathe been captived by Infedyles. [26 May 1588]

Memorandum that a collection was gathered in ow^{er} parish church the viijth day of august anno 1591 by vertue of a lysence for the same grawnted under the Queenes ma^{tie} privie Signet being date the xxiiij day of July anno 1591 grannted to Peter Michaels of Lowrayne a captayn and three others french men captyved by the Turke whose ransomes weare sett at three thousand french crownes and there was gathered for them at this instant tyme the some of six shillings and fower pence half peny farthing the which mony was dellivered unto the said peter his servannt the said day by the hands of Charles Russell and Jhon Woodrose churchwardens in the p^{re}nts [presence] of Thomas Stapleton a scrivener dwelling in Billiter Lane who was his Interpreter.

Collected ... for one william wilch of Cley in the Countie of Norfolke, whose sonne is held Captive in Turkey and was taken in a Shippe called the Long Robert, the somme of xj^s vij^d. [9 February 1616]

Collection in our Church for one William Spalding of Yarmouth in the Isle of Wight, who by Piracie and other losses at Sea lost one Thousand poundes, there was gathered for him xj^s iij^d. [21 December 1617]

Also there was Collected the same day, for one Marie Cooke widow of St Martins parish in the feildes, whose late husband had taken from him by Turkish Pirates the valew of Six hundred poundes, since which time hir sonne was taken prisoner by the Turkes and carried to Argier [Algiers], where he is detained in slaverie, there was gathered for hir xj^s ij^d.

Collection for one John Witheridge and Nicholas Paige Ship-maisters, whose Shipp and goods were taken by Turkish pirates and fiftie men of their Companie sould for Slaves into Barberie . . . one & twentie shillings, and five pence. [25 January 1617]

Gathered . . . for a Grecian Ministere towards the Redeeming his Frends out of Captivitie from amongst the Turkes vij^s i^d. [15 October 1620]

A marginal note adds, "Collection upon the Kings Maties Letters Pattent."

On 21 November 1624 £3 4s. 6d. was collected "for 1500 men helde captive at Argier [Algiers] by the Turkes." This collection also was authorized by letters patent from the king.

The congregation at St. Botolph's concerned itself with prisoners in English as well as Turkish prisons. A collection was taken up on 29 December 1583 for the debtors in the

Marshalsea Prison and on 12 May 1588 for John Hammond, gentleman, in the Fleet Prison. The Bishop of London had issued a license for alms to be collected in the Diocese of London for one year, Hammond being

> in greate extremitie and povertie and in respect of dyvers his good services done unto her ma^tie as well in Ireland as in the Lowe countries.

Three shillings and twopence were collected and "Delivered unto hem ye same Daye."

> A collection for Agnes Browne a Widow having been fyve yeares in prison. [13 August 1598]

Alms were collected on 12 September 1591 by

> vertue of a lysence under the greate seale from the high court of the admiraltie grawnted for the space of six monethes and being dated the vij^th Day of marche 1590 stilo Anglie[27] unto Jhon Kiste of Earmarthen who heare to fore hath bene an owner of good shipping and of good wealth and is nowe of Late by sundrie Losses fallen into utter decay and povertie and being also greatly indebted thereby is comitted prisoner to the marshalsea where he remayneth in great miserie likely to perish unlesse he may be relieved with the Benevolence of charitable persons well disposed to succor his distressed estate. In con-

27. In the English style, that is, about six months earlier. The clerk wanted it to be clear that the suppliant's license was still valid when the collection was taken.

sideration whereof he was grannted to gather in the cittie
of London and the suburbs of the same and the countis of
midlesex kent and surrie and there was gathered for him
. . . the some of two shillings and three pence and the
same beinge ingrosed upon his Briefe was Delivered unto
hem.

One senses a mystery involving Kist, and another about
Hammond. What were the latter's "good services" to Her
Majesty, and why did the Admiralty come to the rescue of
Kist, a former shipowner, now desperate in the Marshalsea?
Perhaps both had rendered important but secret aid to the
Crown and were being discreetly rewarded.

There were lockups, the so-called cages, within the Ward
of Portsoken, but the parish apparently did little to help the
miserable prisoners shut up there. Judging from the numbers
of men, women, and children who died in the cages, we can
assume that they must seldom have gone empty. Babies were
born there and then succumbed, particularly during the winter. Of an illegitimate child that was christened, the clerk
observes that the mother

> was delivered in Cage (a fitt house for such a Ghest . . .).
> God send the Child better grace than hir Parents. [9 Octo-
> ber 1622]

There were cages at Tower Hill,[28] East Smithfield,[29] near

28. 9 February 1585; 14 December 1595; 13 March 1602; 13
and 19 July, 30 August 1603; 20 February 1623.
29. 16 November, 15 February 1609; 5 March 1610; 10 April,
14 September 1618; 12 January 1621.

Whitechapel Bars (14 December 1595), and perhaps in one or two other places in the parish. The inhabitants of the area near Whitechapel Bars did show compassion when on 5 March 1586 they gathered alms

> to relieve sarten sick people in the parish as also to relieve a boye borne in the parish whose toes were rotted off and ded lye in the cadge.

It will be recalled that the offenders listed in the vagrancy laws sometimes included counterfeit "Scollers of the Universityes of Oxford or Cambridge yᵗ goe about begginge." Detection of these rascals required a nice academic distinction, for there were genuine—and equally impoverished—scholars as well. The church took a special collection on 6 September 1584 for "Jhon gibson a skottishman beinge a skoller of Sᵗ Geordges college in cambridge," on 4 June 1587 for "Robert Bawme a Scholler" of Oxford, and on 20 August 1587 for "one Francis worlocke a batchelor of arte in oxford who was become blynde and lame wᵗ imoderate studye." Another unfortunate victim of the expensive pursuit of learning was

> thomas awsten sonn to Jhon awsten Cittizen and haberdasher of london who hathe Bestowed his tyme hetherto in Learning and hathe in the universitie of oxforde proceaded[30] bachelor of Arte. The charge[31] wheare of as also

30. Taken the degree of.
31. Cost.

of Bookes and other things nessesarie for suche a skoller suche as he beinge allredye by the charge of his Late Degree Become Indebted and his Father by pyrates robed and Impoverished is un able to beare for yᵉ wᶜʰ consideracion he was Lysenced by yᵉ bishop of London.

The license, dated 25 February 1586, could be used "wᵗʰ in the dyoses and Jurisdiction of the Sayd Bishop of London." St. Botolph's raised 3s. 8d. for Austin on 19 March 1586, and the money was handed to him by the clerk.

A secret agent for the Crown who had fallen on evil days was rescued, temporarily at least, by the issuance of a license. William Hulls was

a saylor who had beene captyved by the Turk and had beene also used as a spye for England and had receyved dyvers hurtts and maymes by the turke becawse he would not tourne Turk.

His license was awarded to him by the Privy Council. A collection totaling 10s. 5d. was given to him on 31 August 1595 by the minister after the amount had been duly noted on the license.

Hulls was back at St. Botolph's with the same license on 16 January 1596[32] and we learn more about his activities. It is reported that

32. This appears to be the only instance in which the same individual collected twice with one license. Apparently the license was good for more than one year.

since his captivetie under the handes of the Turkes and heathen people [he] verie dutifully and no less faythfully diskovered dyvers and sundrie traytors conspyring against our soveraigne Ladie the Queene, her crowne and dignitie, wherebie there conspyracies have been prevented, and some of the said conspyrators executed w^t condinyne [condign] punishment of which his dutifull & good services benefiting greatlie this our comon wealth, and also in consideration & pittie that he hath lost the use of his left arme, the synewes thereof by the said heathens, Infidells & Turkes most tyranously being cutt for that he would not renownce & deny the Christian fayth and Religion which we all professe, to his utter undoing being destituted of succor & reliefe having a greate charge of wyfe and children.

Hulls's license, it develops, was valid anywhere

w^{t}hin the Realme of England where he shall for his reliefe come and repayre and for & towards the payment of three score and tenn pounds his ransome.

Presumably the ransom had been supplied by another person, and the ex-sailor was now collecting funds to repay his benefactor. St. Botolph's responded handsomely with no less than 9s. 3 1/2d. One suspects that there was much more to the spy's story, but the clerk gives no further details.

Two curious entries reveal donations by the parish to colonists.

Memorandum that on Sunday the xixth day of this month

[October 1617], there was gathered in our Church to-
wardes the plantation of Virginia xix^s and iiij^d.

On Sundaie the xxjst of this Moneth [February 1618],
there was a Collection for Virginia [Colony] being the
third for that purpose, at which there was collected xxv^s.
This Monie was paid to Mr Robert Kemp Register, at his
office.

The Virginia Colony had been founded at Jamestown in
1607. In the absence of any explanation in the parish record, we can guess that the money was collected in response
to a kind of levy by the Crown, perhaps on the grounds that
the colonists were experiencing many hardships.

Probably the most numerous beneficiaries of alms from
St. Botolph's were the indigent sick and handicapped. In one
exceptional case the recipient was a parishioner in the hospital. Francis Pemerton

beinge a poore Boye borne in this parish and nowe beinge
in St. Thomas spittle[33] in suthworke in the hands of surgions and havinge his legge cutt of[f].

On 11 June 1587 the parish collected 6s. for him, the
money being delivered by the constable. Ten days later it was
arranged that Francis would

have alowed him for ye tyme that he shall Lye in the
sayde spittle towarde keepinge and servinge of hem the

33. Hospital.

> some of xij d by the weeke whiche monye shall [be] payd
> unto the mastere of the sayde spittle owte of the sayde
> Lande rentell, that [until] other order be taken for him.

Such an arrangement was rare, probably because it was equally rare for a poor person to gain admission to a hospital. The
land rental came from property owned by the parish.

Again, on 12 May 1588 there was a "collection for the poor
Lame and impotent people in the hospitall of waltham
crosse," a town in Hertfordshire. This was with the authority
of letters patent granted by the Queen to one Thomas Toolye
and valid in Middlesex. Such a collection reflected the inability of the residents of Waltham Cross to pay the full cost of
care for patients in their hospital. As we have seen, the Poor
Laws permitted a community in this predicament to seek elsewhere for help.

When sick persons clearly lacked the resources to support
themselves, the obligation of the parish was clear. Many of
these destitute individuals were former soldiers and sailors.
A collection was taken on 28 April 1588 and again on 12
January of that year for John Darcy "who had received dyvers
hurts and maymes in the queenes Maties warrs in Ireland."
Some other entries concern

> A collection for a mariner of creechurch parishe who Lost
> his hand at the sea in the service of the Queene agaynst y^e
> Spaniards. [11 August 1588]

One Henrie Bunker a souldier who had beene maymed in the queenes ma^tie warre in Ireland. [1 June 1589]

One Nicholas Frengoffe A souldier hurt in the portingale [Portugal] voyadge. [16 November 1589]

One Robert Browne a gunner shott through his bodie and grevously wownded in sondrie other places. [16 November 1589]

Ellis Noble and William bayly sowldiers maymed and hurt. [22 March 1589]

Thomas davis and george adamson too souldiers maymed. [29 March 1590]

Thomas stander A sowldier maymed. [17 April 1590]

On 26 April 1590 there were collections for five soldiers "maymed in ye warrs." William Browne, "a gounner grievously wounded in the service agaynst the spanyards," received alms by virtue of a license from the Admiralty. The document was valid for twelve months.

Jhon Williams a sowldier maymed. [24 January 1590]

Jhon Steele a sayler sore maymed and hurt by the Spanniards. [24 January 1590]

Jhon Bennet a sayler who hadd bothe his Leggs shott of in the princes servis. [31 January 1590]

Jhon Redmund a maymed souldier. [2 February 1590]

George Watkins a maymed souldier. [2 February 1590]

Jhon Davis a sowldier maymed and for Alice his mother.
[16 May 1591]

Jhon Salisburie a sowldier maymed. [12 September 1591]

John Salisbury had been a soldier but had an alms license
for one year from the Court of the Admiralty

under the greate Seale dated the xxxj[th] day of July 1591
and in the three and thirteth yeare of the Raigne of our
Soveraigne Ladie Elizabeth by the grace of god Queene of
England Frannce and Ireland et c.

The clerk went on to say that Salisbury, a Welshman,

of Witherwarne in the cowntie of Merionoth Sowldier
havinge served and being Imployed in her highnes affaires
in france Flanders and on the seas to morocus[34] in the
minnion[35] of London the space of six yeares hath lost the
use of one of his hands and Receyved in his face body and
leggs eleven aparant wownds in curing whereof he hath
spent and consumed all the smale substance he had of him
selfe or cowld any wayes obtayne or gett of his Freends
or others whereby he is browght to suche extremitie and

34. Blurred letters make the spelling of this word uncertain. It
is probably a corruption of *Marruecos,* Spanish for Morocco.
35. The *Minion,* a ship.

distres that he is lyke to perishe unlesse by the meanes of well disposed people he be holped and relieved.

The parish raised 2s. 3d. for him on 12 September 1591. The cryptic reference to Salisbury's employment in the queen's affairs on the high seas and in foreign countries suggests that he too may have been a secret agent.

Alms were also sought by William Jones, a soldier maimed while fighting for six years in Ireland and Flanders. Jones had been granted an "alms roome" in the Cathedral Church of Chester and the further good fortune of a

pasporte to go in to the said contrie for the same under certen of the cownsell[36] there hands dated at Oteland[37] the iiij[th] Day of october Anno 1591 . . . by vertue wheare of there was gathered for him the some of xviij d w[ch] being Ingrosed upon his said pasporte it was delivered unto him. [28 November 1591]

The pathetic procession of disabled soldiers and sailors continued. Among them was Thomas Bricket, formerly a waterman on the Thames,

who haveing served divers of our noble progenetors in the warrs at sondrie tymes and placis upon the seas and therein receyved great Bruses and hurts in his body and limes to his great hindrance.

36. Presumably this meant the Privy Council.
37. I could not identify this place.

Bricket was granted letters patent from the Queen for one year. St. Botolph's found 16d. for him on 10 September 1592, the amount was noted on his license, and the coins were turned over to his wife.

The burden of relief lay heavily on the parish. When Agnes Steele, wife of John Steele, a badly injured sailor, presented his license from the Admiralty, the churchwardens

in consideration of the greate povertie that was in the said parishe of poore men to be relieved by collexions in the parish to [be] gathered and the parish besyde verie muche burthened by lysenses and passports grannted by the Lords of her ma^tie privie cownsell to poore mayned people ded give this xxiij^th day of July anno 1592 [12d.].

This sum was given to Mistress Steele from the poor box. It would seem that another special collection just then would have been too much.

John Steele, wounded by a "great shott" while serving in the Queen's ship *Swallow,* had been granted an alms roam in Thorneton, Lincolnshire. Because he was destitute, he was also given a license to seek alms "for his better sucor and healp in the said journey" north. The license was for two months, probably not too long for an injured man travelling on foot from London.

Service at sea against the Spaniards left John Redman badly wounded and penniless. Since he had a wife and five dependent children, he was awarded both a license to seek alms and an alms room in the Cathedral Church at Norwich. But the room was not yet vacant, and the Redman family came in desperation to St. Botolph's church, which collected 2s. for them on 23 June 1594.

Richard Clarke, another sailor, sought help on 15 June 1595. He had an Admiralty license valid for a year, having

receyved greate hurtes & hinderances by the Dunkerkers at sea and otherwayes in her Maties service to the greate hinderance of him his poore wyfe and thre smale children.

Three shillings and threepence were turned over to him.

On 21 November of the following year there was a collection for William Key, a former trumpeter in Her Majesty's Walloons. He had had "by a greate shott his Ryght arme and part of his syd stroken away to his great hinderance." After this there are no more such entries in the parish record until 20 April 1600, when it is noted that a guild, the Company of Clothworkers, gave some money to an injured soldier. The hiatus is puzzling, since it is hard to believe either that destitute men stopped seeking help or that the clerk gave up recording the donations. After 1600, also, there are practically no entries regarding collections for the needy, but this change reflects a new policy of making entries generally more concise and omitting minor events.

Handicapped soldiers and sailors of course were not the only persons to seek alms from St. Botolph's during the latter part of the sixteenth century. Occasionally a well-to-do parishioner would provide in his will for the distribution of money or food to the poor. Beginning in March 1583 there are almost endless notations about help to needy persons. On the twenty-second of that month

the good wille of ye welldisposed was gathered in ower parishe churche . . . Towarde ye releevinge of too poore men who were greatlye impoverished by ye meanes of longe sicknes.

A collexion for one thomas thornton of hacnye beinge blynde. [2 July 1587]

A collexion for Edward tanner wimbleton burned with fyer. [13 August 1587]

One Mrs Chillester beinge a parishioner visseted w^t sicknes. [27 August 1587]

Six Shillings and fower pence half-penye gathered towards the reliefe of the poore beinge sicke in the parish. [17 September 1587]

For poore sicke people in the parishe. [8 October 1587]

For Jhon Hooke cordwyner hindred by sicknes. [14 July 1588]

For one william stone of high holborne shoe maker whose howse fell downe upon him and bruysed him. [1 April 1589]

For Jhon Williams impoverished by the meanes of a great desease wch his wyfe hath in her head. [26 October 1589]

William Clarke was fortunate enough to have a license to seek alms. He had worked in the Queen's scullery for twenty-five years, until lameness and other infirmities forced him into unemployment and poverty. Now "mynded to travell to the bathe[38] in the countie of Somersett to seke for remedie of his sayd griefes," he was making his slow journey westward. The parish on 15 February 1589 raised 5s. for William.

For one William goldingwater of Holborne a taylor who by the visitation of god had his eyesight taken from him. [20 September 1590]

For henrie courte a cooper in Mrs Woods rents in the Eastsmithfield fallen Lame by the handie worke of god. [17 January 1590]

For Phillip lawrence an old man hindred by an Impediment in his speache. [28 February 1590]

For Edward Sanderson bothe Lame and Impotent. [18 April 1591]

For one Jhon Odwell being a parishioner being a Bursten[39] or dezesed man. [13 June 1591]

38. The city of Bath.
39. Ruptured.

Odwell's burial was recorded on 23 December of the same year.

> For Robert Webster a blynd man. [21 November 1591]

A collection was taken on 28 April 1594

> at the request of one M^{rs} cobhead a widow wyfe to the late deceased M^{r} cobhead a minnester of the word of god and was [because of] her sonne who was to have his legg cutt of.

The churchwardens handed her 10s.

> For David Duffield A blyndman. [8 February 1595]

> For Thomas Whyt a parishioner being sick and in greate need. [14 November 1596]

If a nonresident of the parish became seriously ill while within its boundaries, a lodging was sometimes found for him in a parish home. Such patients were not necessarily indigent. It is not clear whether shelter was provided as an act of compassion or in compliance with a law. In any case, arranging for a bed in someone's home was a partial substitute for care in the almost nonexistent hospitals and was the best that poor people could expect.

> Jerome Allwyght duch skipper belonginge to a ship called the sparrower of midleborowe in Zealand who coming sick from the sayd ship was Lodged at the howse of Garrett Jest a victuler in the parish. [3 February 1589]

Symond [blank space] a dutchman being a hollander who
ded lye sick at the howse of Derick wynen a tipler . . .
dyed of the smale pockes. [5 October 1590]

Thomas Preston, a young bachelor of Buggbrooke in
Northamptonshire, had the misfortune to be caught by a
press-gang, a military detachment that seized men on the
streets and in the taverns and forced them into service in the
army or navy. This outrageous procedure was not at all unusual, and it cost young Preston dearly. He

having beene pressed out for a wayn[40] Dryver under my
lord of Essex for fraunce and being sicke on the other
syd [of] the seas was sent home and being lodged at the
house of Peter Acton cittizen and vintner of London
dwelling at the signe of the three sonnes being as we go
toward the minories where he left his lyfe and was buried
the first day of october 1591 yeares xxiij and being no
parishioner.

A few months later the parish clerk sets down without
comment the sinister story of Mary Parrie, thirty years old
and the wife of a sailor from another parish. This woman

being sicke was taken in to the howse of Reynowld Burnett a laboring man dwelling in hogge lane being in the
libertie of Eastsmithfield wheare the sayd Reynowld had
by the reporte of the neyghbors there aboute the some of

40. A wain, a large heavy wagon or cart.

xiiij^s to keepe her in her sicknes and the said woman
being at the poynt of Deathe he caryed her to the cadge
upon the hill in the said libertie wheare she dyed and after
her sayd death he the sayd Reynowld ded gather certen
money to burie her with but the corps being brought to
the grave he payd the sexten iiij ob[41] towarde his dewtie
and the said Marie was buried the xxijth day of Marche
anno 1591.

The clerk is careful not to make an accusation, but this account raises some questions. If Reynold Burnett had received 14s., a relatively large sum, to care for the sick
woman, why did he carry her to the cage to die? What happened to the balance of the money? Did Burnett collect more
than 4d. for burial fees? If so, it did not go to the clerk in the
usual way, for the record book shows that "nihill" was received for the interment. Only the sexton was paid for his
labor. The whole business seems very dubious indeed, but in
the absence of a coroner's inquest, of any investigative body
to call upon, and indeed of much firm evidence, the clerk
apparently felt that his hands were tied.

Peter Nycholson a singleman or batcheler and as was
sayd he was a sayler being borne at barking in Essex who
being verie sicke in the striete before the signe of the
hartshorne a brewehouse was caried by the head borowe[42]

41. Obols, halfpennies.
42. The headborough was a parish officer who had a constable's
function.

to the house of william Landie a lyghterman dwelling in morlyes rentte . . . where he dyed. [19 December 1594]

Margaret Porter wyfe to henrie porter a fidler. This woman ded lately lye at the howse of Alice Stafford a widow dwelling in pond aley and being sick she [was] tourned from there and being found lying in the striete she was by the officers layed in the cadge being in the libertie of Eastsmithfield where she dyed and was buried the vjth Day of July anno 1595. yeares xxx.

It is not clear whether Mistress Porter was a lodger in the Stafford home before she became ill. In any case she found no compassion at the end. Possibly she showed symptoms of a contagious disease. If, as may well have been the case, she and her fiddler husband were vagrants, no one would care about her.

Mary Stanley a widow of dover as was said a poore woman lyeng sicke at the howse of william prestlie a saylor dwelling in swan aley . . . where she dyed . . . yeares lx. [15 April 1596]

Phillip Navin servant to william camure a silk weaver dwelling in Sugerloafe aley being in the parish of St Katheryne creechurch . . . This stripling being sick was suffered[43] to go abroad in the streete and being neare his end was charitablie taken into the howse or shopp of

---

43. Allowed. The clerk is sarcastic; it was not unusual for masters to drive out servants or apprentices if they became ill.

Danyell Baldgay a parishioner dwelling in the precinct as we go towards the Tower hill where he dyed. [22 February 1596]

Alice Madden wyf to Robert Madden a porter this woman lying sick in the street before the bell[44] dore wth in aldgate was lodged at the howse of Elizabeth Wood a widow dwelling in the grayhound aley . . . where she dyed . . . yeares l. [21 April 1598]

The indigent sick, if they were given shelter at all, usually found it in the homes of humble folk. The latter may have received payment from the parish, but we very seldom see mention of this. The sick and homeless who died in the street were not parishioners.

44. Apparently The Bell was a tavern.

VIII: Web of Days

Our picture of the physical well-being of the Londoner in the reigns of Elizabeth I and James I is of necessity projected, like a photographic print, from negative images of sickness and death. We have seen that, by modern standards, life expectancy in the last part of the sixteenth and first part of the seventeenth centuries was poor. Stillborn deaths were considerably more numerous than in our day. Nine times as many babies died in the first month of life. Of every hundred infants born in the Parish of St. Botolph without Aldgate in the 1580s and 1590s only 70 survived to age one, 48 to age five, and 27 to age ten. Maternal deaths in childbirth were about 100 times what they are now, destroying not only the mothers but the additional children they would have produced. Periodically plague swept huge proportions of the population into hastily dug graves, and between its grim visitations other diseases, largely unchecked, took steady toll. Professional medical care was relatively unskilled and seldom available to the poor. Sanitation was largely nonexistent.

But there were many positive aspects of life in London, even for the less privileged. Births and banns and weddings were noted in great numbers in the parish records. Newly-wed couples trod joyously on the gravestones in the church floor without thought of the dead bones underneath. If many children died, yet their brothers and sisters grew up to become sturdy tradesmen, loyal subjects of the Crown, and the parents of large families. Many illnesses were not fatal. Not everyone was literate, but a good many were, and all could find entertainment and relaxation if they sought them. There was prosperity as well as poverty. The artisans and tradesmen of the parish made and sold silk as well as fustian, corn meal but also comfits, bracelets for those who could afford them and ribbons for those who could not.

Efforts at quarantine were not always successful because the mechanisms of contagion were not understood, but attempts at segregation of plague victims were vigorously pursued and undoubtedly helped. Out of the crude records of death tolls was born the science of biostatistics, great tool of public health workers. The causes and treatment of disease were pondered, if not correctly, at least with an intensity and enthusiasm that would yield results in years to come. And it was, after all, a period of English glory, the age of Shakespeare, Marlowe, and Spenser, of Francis Bacon and Sir

Philip Sidney, of industrial development, the spread of learning, and the warming influence of the Renaissance. The exploits of Drake and Frobisher and Hawkins stirred men's spirits. The Armada went down in defeat and all England rejoiced. Sir Richard Grenville in a single ship, the *Revenge,* battled the entire Spanish fleet. If in ensuing years life under James I seemed dull by contrast, at least it saw the evolution of the common law and the advance and spread of Puritanism, both of them destined to shape England's future profoundly.

As in our own day, national triumphs and achievements stood side by side with gnawing social evils. The web of days include the dark and intermingled threads of poverty, sickness, ignorance, wretched housing, and unwanted dependence that are with us still. The parish record books made clear a familiar pattern of unequal opportunity and of neglect of the weak and unfortunate. Then as now, heavy migrations from rural areas and small towns into a great city failed to solve the problems of the newcomers and exacerbated the difficulties of urban regulation. Unemployment resulted in hunger and lack of shelter; famished, homeless men, women, and children survived as best they could, turning often to mendicancy and crime. Beggars, vagrants, and thieves, whether traveling as individuals or in bands, were rootless and restless. Like the transient if somewhat more fortunate populations of today, they had little interest in contributing to the stability of a community.

Naturally the community, for its part, resented and feared

those who wandered and begged and stole. The poor and homeless disturbed the public conscience as well as the peace. They challenged the law and order that made the community possible. They got their bread by trickery or larceny or abject request instead of by hard work. And they were everywhere in their ragged, dirty, offensive hordes—tramping the streets, sleeping in doorways, even having their babies in church-yards. The hard words bestowed on them in the parish record books undoubtedly reflected the opinions of the congregation.

As we have seen, Parliament repeatedly reacted to the widespread problem by attempting to legislate it out of existence. Harsh laws seem to have brought intermittent improvements, but the regular enactment of new legislation to suppress the vagrancy and roguery is sufficient evidence that punitive laws never really succeeded. The reason, of course, was that they did not strike at the unemployment and its sequelae which produced the rogues and vagrants. Government approached the vexatious problem of social reform only with reluctance—this phenomenon has also been observed in our day—but conceded the need for something better than the lash, the cage, and the branding iron.

With the advent of the Poor Laws some progress began to be made. Slowly it became evident that constructive legislation, even if it did not eliminate poverty and dependency, at least could relieve the victims of these ills. Ways, albeit imperfect ones, were found through which the majority could share in assisting the needy minority, a practice which foreshadowed today's great national programs. However, while the aim was similar to ours, the Elizabethan method was quite different in its mechanism. The national government, instead of itself assuming a large measure of responsibility, delegated most of this to the local churches. The administration of public relief, particularly in the cities, was put in the hands of the parish and its officials.

Such a move was only possible because, as Lunt (1957) points out and the St. Botolph records confirm, the parish had become the elementary unit of administration for the State just as it long had been for the Church. The churchwardens enforced canon law, oversaw the maintenance of the church itself, and collected taxes from members of the congregation when church property needed attention. The overseers of the poor also functioned within the framework of the parish. These officials were elected by the congregation. Parish administration apparently operated fairly smoothly. Finally, the parish church by its very nature was concerned with charitable matters. It was quite natural that Parliament should turn to it for implementation of the Poor Laws.

Each parish was expected to look after its own by raising money and housing orphans and the indigent sick. Strangers in need were to be sent if possible to their own congregations. A notable exception, of course, was made for persons who were licensed to collect alms. As we have seen, they could approach any parish within specified limits of geography and time and expect some assistance. Here again upper levels of government—the Crown, the Admiralty, and so on—prescribed the means and selected the beneficiaries, but the parish provided the funds. As in our times, the government had established a method for relief of the poor, sick, and helpless, and the public, as always, supplied the money. Compulsion, up to and including the threat of a prison sentence imposed by the courts, insured the participation of all who could afford to contribute.

The Elizabethan system for public relief also differed markedly from ours in that the necessary shillings and pence were collected and disbursed within the parish, largely on the basis of specific appeals, and without going through higher levels of government with all the attendant problems of red tape, delay, loss of personal contact, and administrative expense. It is true, of course, that parish efforts were to a degree supplemented by the State, for example, through grants from the Crown to aid a hospital.

Our review of the parish records has left us with some unanswered questions. One concerns the actual numbers of people living through the years in the parish—the population at risk. On the basis of records now known to exist, it is unlikely that this question can ever be answered. Even farther beyond our reach are the actual causes of many of the deaths that were recorded. Correct diagnoses, as we have seen, often were not made; in many cases they were beyond the competence of physicians of that period. A third puzzle lies in the widely different numbers of plague deaths among males and females of certain ages. We can hope that collateral evidence from other parishes may some day untangle this problem.

Nearly four centuries separate us in time from the Londoners of St. Botolph's Parish. The span of their years lies far outside the reality we know, but the inheritance from the men and women of Shakespeare's day has its own immediacy. That extraordinary blend of realism, withdrawal, and kindness, of courage and obstinacy, of humor and stolid acceptance of what life brings seems to characterize the subjects of the second Elizabeth pretty much as it did those of the first. The men, women, and children who elbowed their way in and out of Aldgate, stared at the prisoners in the cages, watched the shipping on the gray Thames, labored in their little shops, strolled the broad meadows of East Smithfield, and went to the parish church on Sunday were not very different from the city dwellers of the twentieth century. The web of days rolls from the loom of time into our hands and, wondering, we see the pattern is unchanged.

Bibliography

Agas, Ralph. 1905. *Plan of London* (circa *1560–1570*) *by Ralph Agas*. London, London Topographical Soc.

Angus, John. 1854. Old and new bills of mortality; movement of the population; deaths and fatal diseases in London during the last fourteen years. *J. Statist. Soc. London, 17*, 117–42.

[Anon.] 1636. *Certain Necessary Directions, As Well for the Cure of Plague, as for Preuenting the Infection.* . . . London, Robert Barker and Iohn Bill [no pagination].

[Anon.] 1665. *London's Dreadful Visitation: or, a Collection of All the Bills of Mortality.* . . . London, E. Cotes [no pagination].

[Anon.] 1937. *The Encyclopaedia Britannica.* London, Encyclopaedia Britannica Co.

[Anon.] 1965. *Vital Statistics of the United States, 1963. Volume II—Mortality, Part A.* . . . Washington, D.C., U.S. Government Printing Office, pp. 1–6, 2–3, 3–4.

[Anon.] 1968. *Demographic Yearbook* ... 1967 ... *Mortality Statistics II*. New York, United Nations, pp. 257–62, 268, 494.

Atkinson, A. G. B. 1898. *St. Botolph Aldgate; the Story of a City Parish*. ... London, Grant Richards, pp. 1, 43, 49, 79, 103, 116.

Barnet, M. C. 1968. The barber-surgeons of York. *Med. Hist.*, *12*, 19–30.

Barron, S. L. 1968. The epidemiology of human pregnancy. *Proc. Roy. Soc. Med.*, *61*, 1200–05.

Bell, John. 1665. *Londons Remembrancer*. ... London, E. Cotes [no pagination].

[Birch, Thomas, ed.] 1759. *A Collection of the Yearly Bills of Mortality, from 1657 to 1758 Inclusive*. ... London, A. Millar, pp. 4, 5, 7, 8, 11, 13, bills.

Blanchard, Rae, ed. 1955. *The Englishman. A Political Journal by Richard Steele*. Oxford, Clarendon Press, 12 Nov. 1713, p. 73.

Bravn, Georgivs, and Franciscvs Hogenbergivs. 1572. Londinvm. In: *Civitates orbis terrarvm*. [Coloniae Agrippinae, svmptibvs avctorvm.] *1* [no pagination].

Brett-James, N. G. 1935. *The Growth of Stuart London*. London, George Allen & Unwin, pp. 248–50, 254–56, 264–66, 534.

Brinkworth, E. R., ed. 1942. *The Archdeacon's Court: Liber Actorum, 1584*. Oxford, Oxfordshire Record Soc., *2*, xvii.

Brown, Theo. 1966. The triple gateway. *Folklore*, *77*, 123–31.

Burn, J. S. 1862. *The History of Parish Registers in England*. ... London, John Russell Smith, pp. 4–6, 11.

Burnet, Gilbert. 1829. *The History of the Reformation of the Church of England*. Oxford, Clarendon Press, *1*, 283.

Christie, James. 1893. *Some Account of Parish Clerks.* . . . London, James Vincent, pp. 132, 135, 138, 141.

Clark-Kennedy, A. E. 1962. *The London; a Study in the Voluntary Hospital System.* . . . London, Pitman, *1*, 1–5.

Clowes, William. 1585. *A Briefe and Necessarie Treatise.* . . . London, Thomas Cadman, fol. 8 recto.

Cock, F. W. 1926. Bills of mortality. *Brit. Med. J.*, *2*, 760.

C[ooper], T[hompson]. 1908. John Graunt. In: Leslie Stephen and Sidney Lee, eds. *Dictionary of National Biography.* New York, Macmillan, *8*, 427–28.

Copeman, W. S. C. 1960. *Doctors and Disease in Tudor Times.* London, Dawson's, pp. 23, 31, 39, 47, 116, 128, 134, 135.

Cowgill, U. M. 1966. Historical study of the season of birth in the City of York, England. *Nature*, *209*, 1067–70.

———. 1970. The people of York. *Sci. Amer.*, *222*, 104–12.

Cox, C. J. 1910. *The Parish Registers of England.* London, Methuen, pp. 1–6, app. 4.

Craig, Hardin. 1932. *Shakespeare.* . . . Chicago, Scott, Foresman, p. 292.

Craigie, W. A., ed. 1914. *A New English Dictionary on Historical Principles.* . . . Oxford, Clarendon Press.

Creighton, Charles. 1891. *A History of Epidemics in Great Britain.* . . . Cambridge, University Press, *1*, 320–22.

———. 1902. Public health. In: H. D. Traill and J. S. Mann, eds. *Social England.* New York, Putnam, *3*, 192–95.

Culpeper, N. 1652. *The English Physician.* . . . London [n.p.], pp. 92, 135.

———. 1657. *Culpeper's Last Legacy.* . . . [London], N. Brooke, p. 30.

Dainton, Courtney. 1961. *The Story of England's Hospitals.* London, Museum Press, p. 33.

Defoe, Daniel. 1920. *Journal of the Plague Year*. London, Dent, p. 7.

Dickens, Charles. 1923. *The Adventures of Oliver Twist*. New York, Macmillan, p. 260.

Ditchfield, P. H. 1907. *The Parish Clerk*. New York, Dutton, pp. 122–23.

Eversley, D. E. C. 1966. Exploitation of Anglican parish registers by aggregative analysis. In: E. A. Wrigley, ed. *An introduction to English historical demography. . . .* New York, Basic Books, pp. 61, 62.

Forbes, T. R. 1966. *The Midwife and the Witch*. New Haven, Conn., Yale University Press, pp. 129–31, 139–41.

Garrison, F. H. 1929. *An Introduction to the History of Medicine. . . .* Philadelphia, Saunders, pp. 237–39, 244, 273.

Gibbons, Peter. 1969. The medical projectors, 1640–1720. *J. Hist. Med., 24,* 247–71.

Glass, D. V. 1963. John Graunt and his *Natural and Political Observations. Proc. Roy. Soc. London,* B, *159,* 2–37.

———. 1966. Introduction. In: *London Inhabitants within the Walls, 1695*. London, London Rec. Soc., pp. vii, xiii, xxiii, xxxvi.

Graunt, John. 1759. *Natural and Political Observations on the Bills of Mortality*. Reprinted from 6th ed., 1676. In: [Thomas Birch, ed.] *A Collection of the Yearly Bills of Mortality, from 1657 to 1758 Inclusive. . . .* London, A. Millar, pp. 1, 6–10, 13–14, 16–17, 22–25, 35, 38, 42.

Graves, Thomas. 1947. *The Story of St. Thomas's; 1106–1947*. London, Faber and Faber, p. 18.

Gray, J. D. A. 1963. *The Central Middlesex Hospital*. London, Pitman, pp. 1–2.

Greenwood, Major. 1948. *Medical statistics from Graunt to Farr. . . .* Cambridge, University Press, pp. 30–32.

Halliwell, J. O. 1847. *A Dictionary of Archaic and Provincial Words....* London, John Russell Smith.

Harben, H. A. 1918. *A Dictionary of London.* London, Henry Jenkins, pp. 93, 349, 481–83.

Hartston, William. 1966. Care of the sick poor in England. *Proc. Roy. Soc. Med., 59,* 577–82.

Hirst, F. L. 1953. *The Conquest of Plague....* Oxford, Clarendon Press, p. 53.

Hollingsworth, T. H. 1968. The importance of the quality of the data in historical demography. *Daedalus, 97,* 415–32.

Jordan, W. K. 1959. *Philanthropy in England, 1480–1660.* ... New York, Russell Sage Foundation, pp. 78, 80, 86–89, 92–93, 96–99.

Kargon, Robert. 1963. John Graunt, Francis Bacon, and the Royal Society: the reception of statistics. *J. Hist. Med., 18,* 336–48.

Lansdowne, Marquis of. 1927. *The Petty Papers....* London, Constable, *1,* 39.

Laughton, J. K. 1909. Sir William Winter. In: Lee, Sidney, ed. *Dictionary of National Biography.* New York, Macmillan, *21,* 691–93.

Law, J. T. 1847. *The Ecclesiastical Statutes at Large....* London, William Benning, *1,* 377–378.

L[ee], S[idney]. 1909. Roderigo Lopez. In: Sidney Lee, ed. *Dictionary of National Biography.* New York, Macmillan, *12,* 132–34.

Lodge, Thomas. 1603. *A Treatise of the Plague....* London, Edward White and N. L. [no pagination].

Lunt, W. E. 1957. *History of England.* New York, Harper, pp. 311–12, 323–24, 357, 383.

MacCulloch, J. A. 1912. Cross-roads. In: James Hastings, ed.

Encyclopaedia of Religion and Ethics. New York, Scribner's, *4,* 330–35.

———. 1922. Vampire. In: James Hastings, ed. *Encyclopaedia of Religion and Ethics.* New York, Scribner's, *12,* 589–91.

McCurrich, H. J. 1929. *The Treatment of the Sick Poor of This Country.* . . . Oxford, Humphrey Milford, p. 5.

McInnes, E. M. 1963. *St. Thomas' Hospital.* London, Allen & Unwin, pp. 14, 20, 22–24, 32.

Mackie, T. T., G. W. Hunter, III, and C. B. Worth. 1954. *A Manual of Tropical Medicine.* . . . Philadelphia, Saunders, pp. 174–85.

Maitland, William. 1756. *The History and Survey of London.* . . . London, T. Osborne, J. Shipton, and J. Hodges, pp. 259, 268.

Manson-Bahr, P. H. 1966. *Manson's Tropical Diseases.* . . . London, Baillière, Tindall & Cassell, pp. 222–35.

Mettler, C. C., and F. A. Mettler. 1947. *History of Medicine.* . . . Philadelphia, Blakiston, p. 549.

Mullett. C. F. 1956. *The Bubonic Plague in England.* . . . Lexington, University of Kentucky Press, pp. 4, 10, 47, 49, 62, 64, 89, 107, 117, 143.

Murray, J. A. H., ed. 1888. *A New English Dictionary on Historical Principles.* . . . Oxford, Clarendon Press.

Neilson, W. A., ed. 1948. *Webster's New International Dictionary.* Springfield, Mass., G. & C. Merriam.

Nicholls, George. 1854. *A History of the English Poor Law.* . . . London, John Murray, *1,* 114–25, 156–69, 181–98.

P[ayne], J. F. 1937. Plague. In: *Encyclopaedia Britannica.* London, Encyclopaedia Britannica Co., *17,* 991.

Phayer, Thomas. 1553. *The Booke of Children.* [n.p., no pagination.]

Phillimore, Robert, ed. 1842. *The Ecclesiastical Law, by Richard Burn.* London, S. Sweet; V. & R. Stevens & G. S. Norton, 2, 423; 3, 112–14, 116, 117.

Phillimore, W. G. F. 1895. *The Ecclesiastical Law of the Church of England.* . . . London, Sweet and Maxwell, p. 528.

Platt, J. C. 1844. Bills of mortality. In: Charles Knight, ed. *London.* London, Charles Knight, 6, 225–40.

Potter, E. L., and F. L. Adair. 1940. *Fetal and Neonatal Death.* . . . Chicago, University of Chicago Press, pp. xiv–xv, 3, 4.

Poynter, F. N. L., ed. 1948. *Selected Writings of William Clowes, 1544–1604.* London, Harvey & Blythe, pp. 12–14.

Quincy, John. 1722. *Lexicon Physico-medicum: or, a New Physical Dictionary.* . . . London, E. Bell.

Ribton-Turner, C. J. 1887. *A History of Vagrants and Vagrancy and Beggars and Begging.* London, Chapman and Hall, pp. 100, 104–07, 114–17, 121.

Roberts, R. S. 1962. The personnel and practice of medicine in Tudor and Stuart England. Pt. I. The provinces. *Med. Hist., 6,* 363–82.

———. 1964. The personnel and practice of medicine in Tudor and Stuart England. Pt. II. London. *Med. Hist., 8,* 217–34.

———. 1966. The place of plague in English history. *Proc. Roy. Soc. Med., 59,* 101–05.

Rosen, George. 1968. Enthusiasm. *Bull. Hist. Med., 42,* 393–421.

Rowse, A. L. 1951. *The England of Elizabeth; the Structure of Society.* New York, Macmillan, pp. 1, 124, 158, 159, 188, 189, 194, 198, 217, 218, 221, 223, 354, 425.

Ryther. 1604. *The Cittie of London.* [n.p.], Stanford's Geogr. Estabt.

Shrewsbury, J. F. D. 1970. *A History of Bubonic Plague in the British Isles.* Cambridge, University Press, p. 17.

Singer, Charles, and E. A. Underwood. 1962. *A Short History of Medicine.* Oxford, Oxford University Press, pp. 179–80.

Smith, Goldwin. 1940. The practice of medicine in Tudor England. *Sci. Monthly, 50,* 65–72.

Stow, John. 1631. *Annales, or a Generall Chronicle of England.* . . . London, Richard Meighen, p. 656.

Strype, John, ed. 1754–55. *A Survey of the Cities of London and Westminster.* . . . London, W. Innys . . . , *1,* 348–71; *2,* 534.

Sutherland, Ian. 1970. Parish registers and the London bills of mortality. *J. Soc. Archivists, 4,* 65.

Tate, W. E. 1951. *The Parish Chest.* . . . Cambridge, University Press, pp. 44–45.

Thoms, W. J., ed. 1842. *A Survey of London, Written in the Year 1598, by John Stow.* London, Whittaker, p. 156.

Thornton, William, *et al.,* revisers. [1793?] *The New, Complete, and Universal History, Description, and Survey of the Cities of London and Westminster.* . . . London, Alex. Hogg, p. 429.

Trotter, Eleanor. 1919. *Seventeenth-Century Life in the Country Parish, with Special Reference to Local Government.* Cambridge, University Press, pp. 1, 3, 59, 164.

Waldo, F. J. 1910–11. The ancient office of coroner. 1. The origin of the coronership. 2. The powers, duties, and qualifications of coroner. *Coroners' Soc. Annu. Rep., 4,* 241–52.

Walford, Cornelius. 1878. Early bills of mortality. *Trans. Roy. Hist. Soc.,* 7, 212–48.

Waters, R. E. C. 1887. *Parish Registers in England.* . . . London, Longmans, Green, pp. 5, 9.

Webb, Sidney and Beatrice. 1927. *English Local Government: English Poor Law History: Part I. The Old Poor Law.* London, Longmans, Green, pp. 48, 51–55, 64, 350, 351.

Wellington, R. H. 1905. *The King's Coroner.* . . . London, William Clowes, pp. 3–9.

Whitteridge, Gweneth, and Veronica Stokes. 1961. *A Brief History of the Hospital of Saint Bartholomew.* London, Governors of the Hospital of Saint Bartholomew, pp. 9, 15.

Williams, D. A. 1960. London Puritanism: the Parish of St. Botolph without Aldgate. *Guildhall Misc.,* 2, 24–38.

Wilson, F. P. 1927. *The Plague in Shakespeare's London.* Oxford, Clarendon Press, pp. 17, 18, 23, 64–66, 72, 73, 90, 91, 106, 114, 167, 174, 175, 187, 189–93, 196, 201, 203, 205–07.

Wright, Joseph. 1903. *The English Dialect Dictionary.* . . . London, Henry Frowde.

Wright, Thomas. 1857. *A Dictionary of Obsolete and Provincial English.* . . . London, Bohn.

Wrigley, E. A. 1966. Family limitation in pre-industrial England. *Econ. Hist. Rev.,* 2nd ser., 19, 82–109.

———. 1968. Mortality in pre-industrial England: the example of Colyton, Devon, over three centuries. *Daedalus,* 97, 546–80.

Zeman, F. D. 1965. The amazing career of Doctor Rodrigo Lopez (?–1594). *Bull Hist. Med.,* 39, 295–308.

Index